FIELD GUIDE
to STAINS

**HOW TO IDENTIFY AND REMOVE VIRTUALLY
EVERY STAIN ON EARTH**

By Virginia M. Friedman, Melissa Wagner,
and Nancy Armstrong

QUIRK BOOKS

PHILADELPHIA

DISCLAIMER

Stains come in all shapes, sizes, and types, and addressing all possible variables when rec-ommending removal tips is difficult. While every care has been taken to test the effectiveness of the information in this book, the author and publisher cannot guarantee results nor take responsibility for any damage resulting from any stain removal method.

Full Library of Congress Cataloging-in-Publication Data available upon request.

ISBN: 978-1-68369-326-0

Printed in China

Typeset in Haboro and Mrs Eaves

Designed by Elissa Flanigan based on a design by Susan Van Horn

Production management by John J. McGurk

Quirk Books

215 Church Street

Philadelphia, PA 19106

quirkbooks.com

10 9 8 7 6 5 4 3 2 1

CONTENTS

FRUITS AND VEGETABLES

MEAT AND PROTEIN

DAIRY PRODUCTS

SAUCES AND CONDIMENTS

BEVERAGES

HOUSEHOLD ITEMS AND MISCELLANY

GARAGE AND YARD

BODILY FUNCTIONS

BATHROOM AND BEAUTY PRODUCTS

INTRODUCTION

No matter how clean, uncluttered, and organized you try to keep your home, stains find a way. Risk factors include eating food, wearing makeup, leaving the house, staying in the house, and having a human body. In other words, it's futile to think you can avoid stains. But with the right tools and knowledge, you can eliminate them one by one. And to eliminate them, you have to understand them.

That's where this guide comes in.

Not all stains are alike, and sometimes the best removal method for one type of stain can actually make another type worse. By learning the habits and habitats of your stains—where they tend to appear, where and when they're usually acquired, and their individual characteristics— you'll be able to choose the best approach to send them packing. You might even be able to prevent that specific stain from coming back. (Although, again, you probably can't banish stains from your life entirely. It's okay! We don't think any less of you.)

The tips on identifying your stain (page 10) will help you start narrowing down the likely culprit. Once you've zeroed in, locate the appropriate section in the field guide, which is conveniently organized by source of stain: fruits and vegetables, meat and protein, dairy products, sauces and condiments, office and school products, and so forth. Individual entries will then tell you where stains tend to hang out, when you might expect to see them, and what to do about them when you find one. And the glossary on page 252 will give you all the background you need on general cleaning techniques and tools.

Stains are a force of nature—and to understand nature, sometimes you need a field guide. Here it is.

STAIN REMOVAL TIPS

☑ Read garment labels before treating any stain.

☑ Use cleaning products according to manufacturer's labels.

☑ Apply stain removers and solutions to the back of a stain; this will push the stain out of the fabric instead of into it.

☑ Treat the stain until it is removed, then discontinue treatment.

☑ Do not apply any kind of heat (including ironing and using the dryer) until you are certain that the stain has been removed. Heat will often set a stain and make it difficult to remove. Instead, allow garments to air dry, then treat again, if needed. Drying stained garments in sunlight is best; it provides some mild bleaching.

☑ Testing for colorfastness is recommended before using any kind of bleach or strong cleaning product. To test, apply the cleaning agent to an inconspicuous area of the garment, such as an inside seam. Steps that include bleaching and may require such a test are indicated in the margin by the universal symbol for bleach, a triangle.

☑ If you have to take a garment to the dry cleaners, point out the stain and explain what it is so that it can be treated accordingly.

☑ Make sure that flammable materials such as turpentine and acetone are completely rinsed from a garment before putting it in the dryer.

HOW TO IDENTIFY YOUR STAIN

Take the guesswork out of stain identification by asking yourself the following questions:

"WHEN DID I LAST WEAR THIS?" Narrowing down the time and place where the stain was acquired will help you figure out just what was spilled.

"HOW COULD THE STAIN HAVE HAPPENED?" Did you sit in it, brush against it, or maybe scuff it with a pant leg? Connecting cause with effect is essential; often, placement of the stain will help identify those mysterious ones.

"WHAT COLOR IS IT?" One of the easiest ways to identify a stain is by its color. But be aware, some stains react differently to different-colored fabrics, while some, like oil, appear colorless at first but darken as dirt clings to them.

"WHAT DOES THIS SMELL LIKE?" Some stains, like alcohol, fruit juices, or motor oil, have unmistakable odors, especially before washing.

ICON KEY

SEASON:

 SPRING

 SUMMER

 FALL

 WINTER

AREAS OF OCCURRENCE:

 TOPS

 TIE

 JACKET

 BOTTOMS

HOME SURFACES

REMOVAL:

 WATER

 BLEACH

 BAR OF SOAP

 LAUNDER

 SPRAY BOTTLE

 IRON

 ABSORBENT

 VACUUM

TEA KETTLE

TEMPERATURE INDICATORS:

• COLD   •• WARM   ••• HOT

FRUITS *and* VEGETABLES

AVOCADO

GENERAL DESCRIPTION: A pear-shaped tropical fruit with a single large pit, skin that ranges from smooth to rough-textured and green to purplish in color, and buttery yellow to green flesh. Avocados have enjoyed an increased visibility in recent years with the widespread popularity of Mexican cuisine. The word "avocado" comes from the Spanish word *aguacate*, which in turn derives from the ancient Aztec word *āhuacatl*, meaning "testicle." Avocados are grown throughout South and Central America and in California, and they have the highest fat content of any fruit.

SEASON: Avocados are a source of stains during any season, but especially the summer barbecue season and at winter and summer sporting events, where guacamole is a popular dip for chips.

AREAS OF OCCURRENCE: Avocado stains normally occur in the standard food-stain places—the fronts of blouses, shirts, and sweaters, and the lap areas of pants, jeans, and dresses. Particularly clumsy or careless people may also find these stains on the seats of their pants, if they don't look before sitting in an "unoccupied" chair.

TIME OF OCCURRENCE: Avocados are popular in salads and sandwiches and wraps often associated with lunch fare, as well as in sauces and dips that are commonly eaten as snacks in the afternoon or evening.

VARIATIONS OF SIGNIFICANCE: Guacamole; any sandwich or wrap with "California" in the name

REMOVAL: 1.   Use a dull knife or spoon to remove as much as possible.

2.   Rub the stain with a liquid enzyme detergent and let stand several minutes, then soak the stain in cold water for 10 to 15 minutes, or until the stain is loosened. Occasionally rub the stained material between thumbs during soaking. Rinse well. Repeat until you have removed as much as possible.

 3.   If the stain remains, apply a laundry presoak (spot stain remover) and let stand several minutes.

4.   Launder in the hottest water safe for the fabric.

BABY FOOD

GENERAL DESCRIPTION: Food with a runny, mashed, no-chewing-necessary consistency, made especially for babies who are just beginning to eat whole food rather than milk. Baby food can be made from just about any fruit or vegetable. Some popular varieties in the United States and Europe include apple, banana, and carrot.

SEASON: Babies must eat year-round, so baby-food stains can happen during any season.

AREAS OF OCCURRENCE: A baby-food stain is frequently found on clothing that surrounds the neck, arms, or chest of the supervising adult. The splatter can range as far away as your back, pants, or socks, depending upon the projectile speed and direction in which the baby flings the food. The baby will most likely be covered in the stuff—the bib, intended to catch most of the food, often ends up being cast aside by the child early in the process, making it one of the cleaner garments. In these cases, baby's dress, shirt, or jumper collects most of the mess.

TIME OF OCCURRENCE: By the time a baby starts eating these more-solid foods, parents are working toward getting the baby on a standard breakfast, lunch, and dinner routine. Baby-food stains will occur during these times, unless the child is particularly obstinate and the parents are indulgent—then there is no telling when this stain might appear.

REMOVAL:

1. Use a dull knife or spoon to remove as much as possible.

2. For fresh stains, soak and agitate the fabric thoroughly in cold water. For dried stains, soak fabric in a mixture of cold water and liquid enzyme detergent for 30 minutes or longer, until the stain is loosened. Rinse well.

3. If the stain remains, rub undiluted liquid enzyme detergent into the stain and let stand several minutes.

4. Launder according to garment label.

5. If the stain remains, soak in enzyme detergent mixture and cold water up to 30 minutes again.

6. Apply a laundry presoak (spot stain remover) and launder again. On white fabrics, bleach any remaining stain by blotting with lemon juice and setting to dry in the sunlight.

BAKED BEANS

GENERAL DESCRIPTION: A dish consisting of cooked navy or great northern beans, pork, onion, molasses or brown sugar, and seasonings. Baked beans are an extremely popular dish in Great Britain. The British, according to surveys, consume twice as many baked beans per capita as Americans do, possibly because baked beans are acceptable at every meal—including and especially breakfast. Baked beans are a favorite at summer picnics and barbecues around the globe.

SEASON: Baked beans are most popular in the summertime. You almost always find a crock of baked beans next to the potato salad and corn on the cob at picnics and barbecues during the summer holidays.

AREAS OF OCCURRENCE: Stains from baked beans normally occur in the standard food-stain areas—in trails on the fronts of blouses, T-shirts, golf shirts, or dresses, and in the lap areas of shorts, jeans, and skirts.

TIME OF OCCURRENCE: Picnics and barbecues, the riskiest times for acquiring this stain, usually take place during the afternoon and early evening hours. However, leftover beans can cause problems late into the night.

REMOVAL:
1. Use a dull knife or spoon to remove as much as possible.

2. Flush the back of the stain immediately with cold water to force the stain through fabric.

3. Rub a liquid enzyme detergent into the stain and let stand several minutes. Rub the fabric between thumbs, then rinse well.

△ 4. Sponge with a mild bleach, such as white vinegar, hydrogen peroxide, or lemon juice, then rinse well.

5. Repeat steps 3 and 4 until no more stain can be removed.

6. Apply a laundry presoak (spot stain remover) and let stand several minutes.

7. Launder with an enzyme detergent. Let garment dry in the sun for added bleaching.

8. If the stain remains, rub an enzyme detergent into the stain and then soak garment in warm water for up to 30 minutes, or until the stain is gone. Rinse well.

9. If the stain remains, apply laundry presoak (spot stain remover) and relaunder.

BEET

GENERAL DESCRIPTION: Commonly known as the garden beet, this firm, bulbous edible root vegetable has leafy green tops, which are also edible and highly nutritious; its color is typically garnet red but can range from pinkish-white to deep red. Also known as red beet and beetroot (especially in Great Britain), or mangelwurzel (a variety of beet used for livestock feed). Beet fans should use caution the next morning, lest their first trip to the bathroom cause a panic about their health.

SEASON:

◎ ☼ ✤ ❄

Beets are available year-round, at salad bars, cafeterias, and restaurants everywhere, and especially in Grandma's kitchen.

AREAS OF
OCCURRENCE:

The chest and lap areas of Sunday-best attire are common for this stain—many churchgoers find beets a tempting commodity at Sunday afternoon salad bars or at the dinner table at Grandma's house.

TIME OF
OCCURRENCE:

Beet stains rarely occur at any time other than between 12:00 p.m. and 2:00 p.m. or from 5:00 p.m. to 7:00 p.m.

VARIATIONS OF
SIGNIFICANCE:

Borscht; pickled beets

REMOVAL:

1. Use a dull knife or spoon to remove as much as possible.

2. Soak a slice of white bread in cold water, then lay it on the stain to absorb the beet juice. Turn the bread over once it is saturated or replace it with another slice of bread.

3. Once the bread has absorbed as much stain as possible, rinse garment with cold water.

4. Apply laundry presoak (spot stain remover) and let stand several minutes.

5. Launder with enzyme detergent according to garment label.

△ 6. If the stain remains, dilute bleach as directed on label and soak the stained garment in it in a non-metal container for 6 to 8 hours or until the stain is removed. Check first for colorfastness. If color is affected, spread garment over a container in the sink and let cold water slowly drip onto the stain. Drain the container as needed. Continue for 3 to 4 hours.

△ 7. If the stain remains, sponge with equal parts hydrogen peroxide and water and lay garment in the sun. Keep moist with peroxide solution until the stain is gone. Test first for colorfastness.

▽ 8. Rinse well. Launder according to garment label.

BROCCOLI

GENERAL DESCRIPTION: Italian for "cabbage sprout"; a member of the cabbage family with a tight cluster (called a curd) of green florets atop a stout, paler green edible stalk. Broccoli is much maligned by children and even some adults—former U.S. President George H. W. Bush refused to eat the vegetable. But broccoli has been popular enough to stick around for nearly two millennia. The Roman naturalist Pliny the Elder described a plant that may have been broccoli (or a close broccoli ancestor) being a popular dish during the first century A.D.

SEASON:

Broccoli can be found at any time of year in take-out Chinese food, homemade casseroles, and any number of other dishes—even as a topping on pizza. The broccoli stain is not limited by season.

AREAS OF OCCURRENCE:	A difficult stain to acquire, it is most likely found on the seat of your pants or possibly on the elbow or fore-arm of a shirt or blouse, if the broccoli is cooked to the point of mushiness. You are more likely to be stained by something coating the broccoli than by the vegetable itself.
TIME OF OCCURRENCE:	Because broccoli probably will not stain unless it is cooked, you will generally get this stain only at meal times, traditionally in the early afternoon or evening.
VARIATIONS OF SIGNIFICANCE:	Casserole; gourmet pizza; stir-fry
REMOVAL:	1. Use a dull knife or spoon to remove as much as possible.
	2. Rinse the stain well with cold water.
	3. Rub the stain with a liquid enzyme detergent and let garment stand several minutes.
	4. Soak in cold water, rubbing the fabric occasionally between your thumbs. Continue soaking and rub-bing until you have removed as much stain as pos-sible.
	5. Rinse well.
	6. If the stain remains, apply a laundry presoak (spot stain remover) and let stand several minutes.
	7. Launder according to garment label.

CABBAGE, RED

GENERAL DESCRIPTION: A variety of the green cabbage, red cabbage is usually small, with dark red-purple waxy leaves that are tougher and slightly more bitter than those of the green cabbage. Red cabbage is a staple in tossed salads, both at home and at restaurants. Baseball player Babe Ruth wore a cabbage leaf under his cap to cool him off while playing—he changed it every two innings.

SEASON:

You run the biggest risk of acquiring such a stain when cutting and preparing cabbage—once it has had the chance to dry out a little, it will rarely cause any problem. Salads including red cabbage are a popular cuisine during the hot summer months, when appetites are small and hemlines are high.

AREAS OF OCCURRENCE:

The forearms and waist areas of shirts and blouses and the fronts of aprons are at greatest risk from a red cabbage stain, as it is most likely acquired when cutting the cabbage head. Other garments have a slim chance of acquiring such a stain, usually transmitted by fingers and hands covered in the juices thoughtlessly brushing the sides of pants or some other piece of clothing.

VARIATIONS OF SIGNIFICANCE: Coleslaw; salads

REMOVAL:

I. Use a dull knife or spoon to remove as much as possible.

2. Rinse the stain well with cold water.

3. Rub the stain with a liquid enzyme detergent and let stand several minutes. Do not be alarmed if the stain changes color.

4. Soak garment in cold water, rubbing occasionally between your thumbs. Continue soaking and rubbing until you have removed as much stain as possible.

 5. Rinse well.

6. If the stain remains, apply a laundry presoak (spot stain remover) and let stand several minutes.

7. Launder according to garment label.

CARROT

GENERAL DESCRIPTION: A member of the parsley family; though the greens are also edible, the word "carrot" will generally mean the plant's tapered root, which is crisp and mild in flavor and often orange (but sometimes purple, yellow, or white) in color. Regardless of the myth popularized by the cartoon rabbit Bugs Bunny, wild rabbits do not favor carrots.

SEASON: Carrot is an ingredient in many foods that are served in any season, including stews and salads. They can also be served on their own as the vegetable portion of dinner or as a snack.

AREAS OF OCCURRENCE: Carrot stains are difficult to acquire. When carrots are cooked whole or served raw, you are more likely to be stained by something coating the carrot than by the vegetable itself. Exceptions are when carrots are served as baby food (see Baby Food on page 15) and are pureed for soups, sauces, or juices. They are then most likely found on the seat of your pants or possibly on the elbow or forearm of a shirt or blouse.

VARIATIONS OF
SIGNIFICANCE: Carrot cake; coleslaw; salads; soups

REMOVAL 1. Use a dull knife or spoon to remove as much as possible.

2. Rinse the stain well with cold water.

3. Rub the stain with a liquid enzyme detergent and let stand several minutes.

4. Soak garment in cold water, rubbing the stain occasionally between your thumbs. Continue soaking and rubbing until you have removed as much stain as possible.

5. Rinse well.

6. If the stain remains, apply a laundry presoak (spot stain remover) and let stand several minutes.

7. Launder according to garment label.

FRUITS OR BERRIES

GENERAL
DESCRIPTION: FRUITS: The edible organs that develop from the ovary of flowering plants and contain one or more seeds; usually sweet and eaten as is or processed into other foods. BERRIES: Imprecisely used term to describe any small, juicy fruit that grows on a vine or bush and generally has a thin skin, multiple small to tiny

seeds, and a sweet flavor. Fruits and berries comprise any number of foods, such as peaches, pears, apples, strawberries, blueberries, raspberries, blackberries, oranges, grapes, melons, plums, pomegranates, and cranberries. Botanically speaking, a "true" berry has seeds on the inside, not on the outside. Therefore, "true" berries include the grape, tomato, and eggplant but not the raspberry, blackberry, or strawberry. For our purposes, this category of stain encompasses all varieties commonly referred to as "fruits" or "berries," regardless of exact definition.

SEASON:

You cannot relax your vigilance against this stain in any particular season, as you may encounter the juice or flesh of a fruit or berry at any time of year. There is an increased chance of stain during summer, when numerous fruits and berries are in season locally, depending on your climate.

TIME OF OCCURRENCE:

Fruits and berries are eaten throughout the day, and can therefore stain at any time. Pay careful attention when sipping juice, putting berries on cereal, or eating grapefruit at breakfast, when snacking on an apple, an orange, or a bunch of grapes to boost energy midday, or when devouring a strawberry or cherry pie for dessert after dinner.

VARIATIONS OF SIGNIFICANCE:

Desserts, especially in pies, in cobblers, and over ice cream; juices; in some entrees and soups; on cheese plates; wine (see Wine, Red on page 116; Wine, White on page 118)

REMOVAL: *For fresh stains on fabric:*

1. Treat the stain as soon as possible. Use a dull knife or spoon to remove as much as possible. If you cannot treat the stain immediately, sprinkle it with salt.

2. Rinse any remaining stain well with cold water.

3. Rub liquid laundry detergent into the stain. Do not use bar or natural soap of any kind on the fabric or the stain will set.

4. Let stand several minutes, then rinse the back of the stain well in hot water, letting the water pass quickly through the fabric.

5. If the stain remains, stretch the stained fabric stain side down over a basin. Boil three or more cups of water in a pot or teakettle and carefully pour over the stain from a height of 1 to 2 feet. (This may require two people: one to hold the fabric taut and the other to pour the water.) This procedure will force the stain through the fabric. If you're the only one on stain duty, run the faucet water as hot as possible and carefully hold the stain under it.

6. If the stain remains, apply a laundry presoak (spot stain remover) and launder with liquid enzyme detergent.

7. If the stain remains, sponge it with a light bleach solution, such as equal parts white vinegar and water. Rinse well and let dry in sunlight. Repeat as needed until no more stain can be removed.

8. Apply laundry presoak and relaunder with enzyme detergent.

9. If the stain remains, rub enzyme detergent into the stain and soak in water up to one hour or until the stain is removed. Rinse well and launder.

For dried stains on fabric:

1. Make a paste of borax and water (at a ratio of approximately 3 to 1) and spread onto the stain.

2. Let stand 15 minutes, then rinse. If borax is not available, rub glycerin into the stain and let stand for one hour. Rinse.

3. See steps 3 through 9 for fresh stains, above.

JAM OR JELLY

GENERAL DESCRIPTION: JAM: **A preserve of slightly crushed fruit boiled with sugar.** JELLY: **A sweet spread of fruit juice boiled with sugar and sometimes pectin, then cooled to a soft, sticky consistency.** The primary difference between a jam and a jelly is that a jam has fruit bits in it, since the whole fruit is boiled for preparation. Popular varieties of these breakfast treats include grape, strawberry, and orange marmalade.

SEASON:

Jam and jelly are preserved, so these stains aren't limited to summer, when most fruits and berries are available. Jam-filled cookies and cakes may be more common during the winter holiday season, but jam itself is a stain source you'll find year round.

AREAS OF OCCURRENCE:	The front of a blouse, jacket, or pair of pants is the most likely spot you'll encounter this stain. Jam and jelly have a particularly plop-prone consistency, thus there is little chance of escaping this stain once the substance has been set in motion.
TIME OF OCCURRENCE:	The most common time of day for this stain is probably morning, at breakfast, though lunchtime and dessert are also popular times to consume this sweet treat.
VARIATIONS OF SIGNIFICANCE:	Peanut butter and jelly sandwiches; jam-filled cookies and cakes
REMOVAL:	*For fresh stains on fabric:*

1. Treat the stain as soon as possible. Use a dull knife or spoon to remove as much as possible. If you cannot treat the stain immediately, sprinkle it with salt.

2. Rinse any remaining stain well with cold water.

3. Rub liquid laundry detergent into the stain. Do not use bar or natural soap of any kind on the fabric or the stain will set.

4. Let stand several minutes, then rinse the back of the stain well in hot water, letting the water pass quickly through the fabric.

5. If the stain remains, stretch the stained fabric stain side down over a basin. Boil three or more cups of water in a pot or teakettle and carefully pour over the stain from a height of 1 to 2 feet. (This may require two people: one to hold the fabric taut and the other to pour the water.) This pro-

cedure will force the stain through the fabric. If you're the only one on stain duty, run the faucet water as hot as possible and carefully hold the stain under it.

6. If the stain remains, apply a laundry presoak (spot stain remover) and launder with liquid enzyme detergent.

7. If the stain remains, sponge the stain with a light bleach solution, such as equal parts white vinegar and water. Rinse well and let dry in sunlight. Repeat as needed until no more stain can be removed.

8. Apply laundry presoak and relaunder with enzyme detergent.

9. If the stain remains, rub enzyme detergent into the stain and soak in water up to 1 hour, or until the stain is removed. Rinse well and launder.

For dried stains on fabric:

1. Make a paste of borax and water (at a ratio of approximately 3 to 1) and spread onto the stain.

2. Let stand 15 minutes, then rinse. If borax is not available, rub glycerin into the stain and let stand for 1 hour. Rinse.

3. See steps 3 through 9 for fresh stains, above.

LEMON JUICE

GENERAL DESCRIPTION: The juice of the lemon, a yellowish, acidic citrus. Lemon juice is useful not only as a food item or flavoring; it can be used to lighten hair in the summertime. In addition to being a source of stains, it also works as a stain-removing agent. It can be used to get rid of lipstick stains on white or colored garments, though it must be diluted with water for this purpose. (See Lipstick on page 214.)

SEASON:

While lemon juice is used as a flavoring in recipes throughout the year, summer is the most likely time for this stain to appear. Fish and seafood are often served in summer with a lemon wedge, and lemonade is a favorite summertime refreshment. As previously mentioned, lemon juice is a natural hair-lightener when applied on a hot, sunny day.

AREAS OF OCCURRENCE:

Juice from a squeezed lemon can squirt just about anywhere, from your eyes to your shoes. Therefore, these stains are not limited to any specific area of clothing, though perhaps the front and sleeves of a blouse or T-shirt are the most vulnerable.

VARIATIONS OF SIGNIFICANCE:
Fish and seafood condiment; lemonade; vinaigrette

REMOVAL:
On fabric:

1. Rinse the back of the stain immediately and thoroughly with cold water to neutralize the acid.

2. Place garment on an absorbent cloth and sponge well with ammonia, starting from the outside of the stain edge. Replace cloth underneath as it becomes saturated. (If treating stains on wool or silk, dilute ammonia with an equal amount of cold water.) If ammonia is not available, substitute a bak-

ing soda paste, mixing baking soda and water (at a ratio of approximately 3 to 1). Rub into the stain.

3. Rinse well.

4. Repeat as needed.

5. Launder according to garment label.

On carpet:

1. Sponge the stain immediately with cold water to remove as much acid as possible.

2. Mix baking soda and water to make a paste (at a ratio of approximately 3 to 1) and rub onto the stain. Scrub into carpet with an old toothbrush, then let dry.

3. Repeat steps 1 and 2 until you have removed as much stain as possible.

4. Vacuum.

ONION, RED

GENERAL DESCRIPTION: A plant in the amaryllis family with an edible, pungent bulb; a staple in all kinds of cookery. Commonly used in savory dishes for flavor, red onions are found on most menus, in dishes ranging from salads to burritos. Their flavor comes largely from their aroma; apple, onion, and potato all have the same taste, but the difference is in their smells. To prove this, perform a taste test. Pinch your nose and take a bite of each; they all taste sweet.

SEASON: ⚙ ☼	Since red onions are most common in warm-weather foods, such as pasta salad and salsa fresca, this stain is more prevalent in summer, especially at barbecues. However, since you may crave a slice on a hamburger in winter, these stains won't be limited to the hot months of the year.
AREAS OF OCCURRENCE: 👖	The lap areas of pants, shorts, skirts, and sundresses are the most likely spots for this stain to show up. The fronts of swimsuits and bathing trunks are not exempt, due in large part to the proximity of pools to grills in backyards across the country.
TIME OF OCCURRENCE:	This is one stain that will almost never appear on clothing early in the morning, though the occasional Spanish omelet might provide the exception to this rule. Lunchtime and evening are the most common times to incur this stain.
VARIATIONS OF SIGNIFICANCE:	Burritos; hamburgers; pasta salad; salsa; tacos
REMOVAL: 💧	1. Use a dull knife or spoon to remove as much as possible. 2. Rinse the stain well with cold water. 3. Rub the stain with a liquid enzyme detergent and let stand several minutes. Do not be alarmed if the stain changes color. 4. Soak garment in cold water, rubbing it occasionally between your thumbs. Continue soaking and rubbing until you have removed as much stain as possible.

5. Rinse well.

6. If the stain remains, apply a laundry presoak (spot stain remover) and let stand several minutes.

7. Launder according to garment label.

PEPPER, RED/GREEN/YELLOW

GENERAL DESCRIPTION: The fruit of any of several plants in the genus *Capsicum*, which may be mild to extremely hot. Found in cuisines as varied as Chinese, Mexican, Italian, and Indian, peppers can contain up to three times as much vitamin C as oranges. Mild peppers contain more vitamin C than their hot counterparts. The "heat" comes from the alkaloid ingredient capsaicin; spicy peppers contain more of this substance than mild ones. Climate, location, and age determine the amount of capsaicin in a pepper. To grow really hot peppers, the temperature at night must stay warm; the longer a pepper is left on the vine, the more capsaicin it will contain, and the hotter it will be.

SEASON: Like onions, peppers are common in summertime foods, such as pasta and green salads, as well as in Mexican treats, such as quesadillas and enchiladas. Given their intense flavor and their popularity as a pizza topping, however, this stain is not limited to summer.

AREAS OF OCCURRENCE: There is not much chance you'll find this stain on the back of a jacket or pair of trousers, though the errant pepper could find its way onto a lawn chair. Again, like onions, pepper stains will most commonly be found on the fronts of T-shirts, shorts, and jeans.

<table>
<tr><td>VARIATIONS OF SIGNIFICANCE:</td><td>Enchiladas; marinara sauce; stir-fry; salads</td></tr>
</table>

REMOVAL:

1. Use a dull knife or spoon to remove as much as possible.

2. Rinse the stain well with cold water.

3. Rub the stain with a liquid enzyme detergent and let stand several minutes.

4. Soak garment in cold water, rubbing it occasionally between your thumbs. Continue soaking and rubbing until you have removed as much stain as possible.

5. Rinse well.

6. If the stain remains, apply a laundry presoak (spot stain remover) and let stand several minutes.

7. Launder according to garment label.

POTATO, SWEET

GENERAL DESCRIPTION: The sweet, bright-orange-fleshed tuber of fall and winter that grows on the Central American trailing vine *Ipomoea batatas*; a member of the morning glory family. These potatoes are tasty when prepared the ways you would prepare white potatoes and winter squash—fried, mashed, roasted, or baked. Although "yam" and "sweet potato" are often used interchangeably, they are, in fact, two entirely different vegetables. Yams have dark, scaly skin, while sweet potatoes have a thin, smooth skin.

SEASON:

Since this vegetable is at its best in fall and winter, these are the seasons you'll find its stain on your clothing. Pies and casseroles made with the tuber will have you wondering what to do with the burnt-orange stain on your favorite woolly sweater.

AREAS OF
OCCURRENCE:

Winter clothing is bulky by nature, thus sweater sleeves often are dragged through bowls of food, especially at crowded family gatherings where there is a veritable cornucopia of foodstuffs. Other common spots to find this stain are the fronts of jeans and corduroys, or the lapels of a casual suit jacket.

TIME OF
OCCURRENCE:

This stain will appear in the evening or late afternoon. There is little chance of a sweet-potato stain occurring in the morning, though leftover pie certainly makes a tasty breakfast.

VARIATIONS OF
SIGNIFICANCE:

Potato pancakes; pumpkin and sweet-potato soups; sweet-potato pie

REMOVAL:

1. Use a dull knife or spoon to remove as much as possible.

2. For fresh stains, soak and agitate the fabric thoroughly in cold water. For dried stains, soak fabric in a soapy mixture of cold water and liquid enzyme detergent for 30 minutes or until the stain is loosened. Rinse well.

3. If the stain remains, rub a liquid enzyme detergent into the stain and let stand several minutes.

4. Launder according to garment label.

5. If the stain remains, soak in enzyme detergent and cold water mixture for up to 30 minutes.

6. Apply a laundry presoak (spot stain remover) and launder again. On white fabrics, bleach any remaining stain by blotting with lemon juice and setting to dry in the sunlight.

SPINACH

GENERAL DESCRIPTION: A plant cultivated for its dark green leaves, which are eaten as a vegetable. One of the first cooking greens to appear in spring, spinach is a vegetable found in the traditional foods of nations around the globe. Although it's true that spinach is rich in iron, it also contains oxalic acid, which binds to the iron, allowing less than 5 percent of it to reach the body. However, spinach is also an excellent source of beta-carotene.

SEASON: A stain caused by fresh spinach is most likely to occur in spring or summer, but a frozen-spinach stain can happen at any time of year.

AREAS OF OCCURRENCE: After eating spinach dishes, you may discover a stain anywhere from the fronts and sleeves of shirts to the legs of trousers and fronts of skirts. A more common type of spinach stain, however, occurs when a parent or guardian is feeding creamed or pureed spinach to a baby. In this situation, the green stuff can be found in such far-reaching spots as socks and headbands, or even the insides of garments.

VARIATIONS OF SIGNIFICANCE:	Spinach salad; creamed spinach; eggs Florentine; spanakopita

REMOVAL:

1. Use a dull knife or spoon to remove as much as possible.

2. Place garment stain side down on absorbent cloth and sponge the back of the stain with rubbing alcohol, replacing pad underneath as needed. Test first for colorfastness. (For acetate fabrics, dilute alcohol with 2 parts water. Do not use alcohol on wool.) Rinse well in cold water.

3. If the stain remains, use an old toothbrush and scrub the stain with non-gel toothpaste (preferably containing baking soda). Let stand for 2 to 3 minutes. Rinse well. If toothpaste is not available, sponge the stain with white vinegar, then rinse well.

4. If the stain remains, repeat steps 1 through 3 until you've removed as much stain as possible.

5. Rub the stain with laundry presoak (spot stain remover) and let stand for several minutes.

6. Launder with a liquid enzyme detergent.

SQUASH

GENERAL DESCRIPTION:	The fruit of any of the edible species of the genus *Cucurbita*, squash is treated as a vegetable in the kitchen. The name doesn't come from the verb "squash," which means to crush; instead, it comes from the Narraganset *askútasquash*, meaning "vegetable eaten green."

Squash is most often considered a summer fruit—hence "summer squash"—though there are winter squash ripening along with pumpkins and sweet potatoes. Given these seasonal varieties, this is a stain that occurs primarily in summer and winter.

VARIATIONS OF SIGNIFICANCE:

Ratatouille; stir-fry

REMOVAL:

1. Use a dull knife or spoon to remove as much as possible.

2. Rinse the stain well with cold water.

3. Rub the stain with a liquid enzyme detergent and let stand several minutes.

4. Soak garment in cold water, rubbing it occasionally between your thumbs. Continue soaking and rubbing until you have removed as much stain as possible.

5. Rinse well.

6. If the stain remains, apply a laundry presoak (spot stain remover) and let stand several minutes.

7. Launder according to garment label.

TOMATO

GENERAL DESCRIPTION:

Often thought of as a vegetable, the popular tomato is actually a fruit. A fruit is classified as the edible part of the plant that contains the seeds, while a vegetable is the stems, leaves, and root of the plant. Specifically, in fact, the tomato is a berry (a subset of fruit). Until the late eighteenth century, many cultures, including the British, considered the tomato unsuitable as a food because it was thought to be poisonous due to its relation to the deadly nightshade. This myth eventually died out among United States colonists, and by the early nineteenth century, tomatoes were a necessary ingredient across the country, from Louisiana Creole cooking to Manhattan clam chowder.

SEASON:
☀

Though the growing season for tomatoes is very short—from spring in the American South to mid-fall in the North—the tomato is a staple that is enjoyed throughout the year because it is easily and well preserved in cans. Fresh tomatoes are more likely to stain clothing in the summer, but stewed, pureed, or canned tomatoes will stain all year round.

AREAS OF OCCURRENCE:

The juice, pulp, and seeds of the tomato have an unrivaled ability to squirt unexpectedly, landing on unsuspecting clothing and upholstery. Therefore, all clothing is vulnerable to a tomato stain.

TIME OF OCCURRENCE:

Tomato consumption has no prescribed time. From omelets in the morning to bacon-lettuce-and-tomato sandwiches in the afternoon to an Italian feast in the evening, tomato stains are ubiquitous.

VARIATIONS OF SIGNIFICANCE:

Bruschetta; burritos; chili; gazpacho; jambalaya; marinara sauce; pizza; ratatouille; salads; salsa; tacos; tomato soup

REMOVAL:

I. Use a dull knife or spoon to remove as much as possible.

2. Flush the back of the stain immediately with cold water to force stain through fabric.

3. Rub a liquid enzyme detergent into the stain and let stand several minutes. Rub the fabric between thumbs, then rinse well.

4. Sponge with a mild bleach, such as white vinegar, hydrogen peroxide, or lemon juice, then rinse well.

5. Repeat steps 3 and 4 until no more stain can be removed.

6. Apply a laundry presoak (spot stain remover) and let stand several minutes.

7. Launder with an enzyme detergent. Let garment dry in the sun for added bleaching.

8. If the stain remains, rub an enzyme detergent into the stain and then soak garment in warm water for up to 30 minutes, or until the stain is gone. Rinse well.

9. Apply laundry presoak (spot stain remover) and relaunder.

ZUCCHINI

GENERAL DESCRIPTION: An elongated summer squash with smooth, dark green skin that is a member of the cucumber and melon family. This squash is at its best when ripe and firm. Those who choose to plant this squash should check with friends first; zucchini plants produce far more fruit than one family can consume in a summer.

SEASON:
☀
Since zucchini is a summer squash, the stains from this vegetable invariably appear in the warmest months of the year.

AREAS OF OCCURRENCE:
👖
Given this vegetable's popularity at barbecues, and the popularity of spirits at those same barbecues, zucchini stains can appear on any and all areas of clothing, including bathing-suit straps and the seat of a favorite pair of Capri pants.

VARIATIONS OF SIGNIFICANCE:
Pasta salads; polenta; ratatouille; stews

REMOVAL:

1. Use a dull knife or spoon to remove as much as possible.

2. Rinse the stain well with cold water.

3. Rub the stain with a liquid enzyme detergent and let stand several minutes.

4. Soak garment in cold water, rubbing it occasionally between your thumbs. Continue soaking and rubbing until you have removed as much stain as possible.

5. Rinse well.

6. If the stain remains, apply a laundry presoak (spot stain remover) and let stand several minutes.

7. Launder according to garment label.

MEAT *and* PROTEIN

———

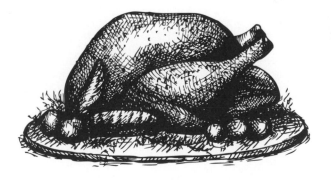

EGG

GENERAL DESCRIPTION: The ovum of an animal—or, in the context of something you're likely to be stained by, specifically the unfertilized ovum of a domesticated fowl. The chicken egg might just be the most important food in the kitchen (at least if you aren't vegan), since it contains all nine essential amino acids as well as several vitamins. Many of our favorite foods would be unrecognizable without the egg, from breakfast to dessert to baked goods of all kinds. Though most eggs are white or brown, some breeds of chickens lay other colors of eggs. For example, Ameraucana and Araucana chickens can lay eggs in shades of blue or green.

SEASON: Given the egg's wide-ranging uses—from sauce thickener to quiche base to pizza topping (in Australia)—you'd be hard-pressed to find a season in which you wouldn't run the risk of an egg stain. Due to the high volume of dessert baking that is done during the holiday seasons, you might encounter this stain more often in November and December.

AREAS OF OCCURRENCE:

Since a raw egg is gooey and has the tendency to splash a bit, its stain location is likely to be as diverse as its many uses, appearing on both shirts and slacks, as well as aprons, bibs, skirts, and blazers. Ties, too, are not immune to this stain, as breakfast before work can be a hurried affair.

TIME OF OCCURRENCE: The aforementioned breakfast is a common time to suffer this stain, though the offense isn't limited to the morning by any means. Since the baking of cookies, cakes, and pies may occur at any time during the hysteria accompanying holiday preparations, an egg stain likewise knows no particular time frame.

VARIATIONS OF
SIGNIFICANCE:
Cake and pancake batter; cookie dough; egg salad; frittatas; omelets; pie crust; quiche; salads

REMOVAL:
1. Use a dull knife or spoon to remove as much as possible. Blot remaining stain with an absorbent cloth.

2. Sponge the stain with cold water, then rinse the back of the stain well. Dried stains may need to be loosened by rubbing with a liquid enzyme detergent and soaking in cold water until the stain begins to break down. Rub the stain between your thumbs while soaking. Rinse well.

3. If the stain remains, rub liquid enzyme detergent into the stain again and let stand for several minutes.

4. Launder according to garment label.

FATS, ANIMAL

GENERAL
DESCRIPTION:
The adipose tissue of an animal, probably one being used for food, though fats may also feature in some candles and cleaning products. Used principally in the body to store energy from food eaten in excess of need. Animal fats serve a huge array of purposes. Not only adding flavor to steaks, roasts, hamburgers, and bacon, they are an essential ingredient in crayons and some soaps. Though the cholesterol-conscious (and,

of course, vegetarians) try to avoid eating animal fats as much as possible, any chef, from Grandma to Bobby Flay, knows that a little bit of fat can mean a whole lot of flavor.

SEASON:

For carnivores, the season is always right for a slice of bacon, a juicy hamburger, or a thick steak. The month of January, just after New Year's resolutions are set, might be the one time of year that these stains are less likely to occur.

AREAS OF OCCURRENCE:

Lard and other animal fats don't migrate toward one particular staining area—any available surface is fair game. When tending the grill during summer barbecues, keep attention focused on T-shirts and shorts, which all too easily fall prey to a renegade hot dog or Polish sausage. Diner employees and patrons run an especially high risk to their aprons and clothes—diners are called "greasy spoons" for a reason.

TIME OF OCCURRENCE:

Animal fats never rest—with bacon at breakfast, deli sandwiches at lunch, pot roast at dinner, and pepperoni pizza as a midnight snack, a greasy animal-fat stain might appear at any time of the day or night. This stain is particularly tricky to detect in low lighting, and may escape notice until hours, days, or even months after the stain is acquired, especially if the clothing is retired to the closet after a night out and not washed immediately.

REMOVAL:

On fabric:

1. Use a dull knife or spoon to remove as much as possible.

2. Apply a laundry presoak (spot stain remover), and let stand for several minutes to allow it to penetrate fabric.

3. Rub liquid enzyme detergent into the stain and let stand several minutes, then launder in hottest water safe for fabric.

On wallpaper:

1. Use a dull knife or spoon to remove as much as possible.

2. Place a sheet of absorbent paper, such as a paper towel or brown paper bag (ink side up), over the stain and press with a warm iron. Replace the absorbent paper once saturated.

3. If the stain remains after pressing, make a paste of cornstarch or baking soda and water (at a ratio of approximately 3 to 1), and smear it on the stain.

4. Let the paste dry, then brush it off.

5. Repeat as necessary.

6. Apply a laundry presoak (spot stain remover) and let stand several minutes.

7. Wipe off with a damp cloth.

8. Repeat as necessary.

On carpet:

1. Sprinkle with an absorbent powder such as baking soda or talcum powder. Let stand several hours.

2. Vacuum.

3. If the stain remains, shampoo with a liquid carpet detergent according to manufacturer's directions. Or sprinkle with dry carpet-cleaning powder, let stand several hours, then vacuum.

HUMMUS

GENERAL DESCRIPTION: A dip made from mashed chickpeas, tahini, lemon juice, garlic, and olive oil. Chickpeas (also known as garbanzo beans), the primary ingredient in hummus, are even older than pottery—archaeologists have found domesticated chickpeas that date back more than ten thousand years. A staple in Middle Eastern cuisines, hummus has gained tremendous popularity in the West as a dip for vegetables and breads, especially in communes and in urban areas with natural-food grocery stores.

AREAS OF OCCURRENCE:

Making generalizations regarding the trajectory of hummus is difficult due to its varying consistencies. If it has a runny texture (a high proportion of tahini and oil), its stain might appear on the fronts of sweaters, shirts, T-shirts, or blouses, as well as on the lap areas of pants. If the hummus is thick (mostly mashed chickpeas), you run less risk from its dripping and more from your sitting on a plate of hummus and vegetables at a party or a barbecue where hors d'oeuvres are served.

VARIATIONS OF SIGNIFICANCE: Falafel sandwiches; wraps

REMOVAL: 1.   Use a dull knife or spoon to remove as much as possible.

2.   Apply a laundry presoak (spot stain remover), and let stand for several minutes.

3.   Rub liquid enzyme detergent into the stain and let stand several minutes.

4.   Launder in the hottest water safe for the fabric.

PEANUT BUTTER

GENERAL DESCRIPTION: A paste made from ground roasted peanuts, vegetable oil, sugar, and salt; available in smooth and chunky styles, as well as natural, which contains no added sugar, oil, or salt. For those who aren't allergic to nuts, peanut butter is a food that often inspires a wave of nostalgia. Ever since it was introduced to an ecstatic crowd at the Universal Exposition in 1904, peanut butter has been all the rage, with kids and adults alike, although the precipitous rise in childhood peanut allergies means some people must seek their hit through alternatives like almond butter.

SEASON: Peanut butter's popularity is at its peak while school is in session, but it is active year-round as a flavoring for desserts and as a topping on toast at breakfast time.

AREAS OF OCCURRENCE: Walls, furniture, carpets, socks, shoes, pants, shirts, dresses, hats—there is no limit to the areas that might be affected by a peanut butter stain, especially when a young child is involved.

TIME OF OCCURRENCE:	Peanut butter is a food that can be served morning, noon, and night, but stainings are most probable between 11:30 a.m. and 1:00 p.m. in a grade-school cafeteria.
VARIATIONS OF SIGNIFICANCE:	Cookies; ice cream; peanut butter and banana sandwiches; peanut butter and jelly sandwiches; peanut butter and marshmallow sandwiches; pies
REMOVAL:	1. Use a dull knife or spoon to remove as much as possible.
	2. Apply a laundry presoak (spot stain remover) and let stand for several minutes to allow it to penetrate fabric.
	3. Rub liquid enzyme detergent into the stain and let stand several minutes.
	4. Launder in the hottest water safe for the fabric.

TUNA FISH

GENERAL DESCRIPTION:	The meat of a fish from the family *Scombridae*, including the albacore, bluefin, and yellowfin. Tuna is one of the few types of fish that may be more popular canned than fresh. These fish swim at a steady rate of nine miles per hour for an indefinite period of time—they never stop moving, for they need a continuous flow of water across their gills to breathe. A tuna that lives to fifteen years old may travel over a million miles in its lifetime.
SEASON:	Due to the popularity of canned tuna, this stain may appear in any season. From sandwich filling (when

mixed with ingredients like mayonnaise, pickles, onions, and celery) to the sometimes-dreaded dinner staple tuna casserole, tuna will stain perennially. (See Oil, Cooking or Vegetable on page 86; Mayonnaise on page 82.)

AREAS OF OCCURRENCE: Tuna is one stain that won't usually travel very far, as it is rarely runny or capable of being splatter ed. You will usually encounter a tuna stain on the fronts of trousers, shorts, dresses, jackets, and sweaters.

TIME OF OCCURRENCE: A tuna stain will hardly ever occur in the morning, as there is little chance of it being used in omelets or as a cereal topping. This fish is not a particularly popular midnight snack, either, and so afternoon and evening are the most likely times for a tuna stain to develop.

VARIATIONS OF SIGNIFICANCE: Niçoise salad; tuna casserole; tuna salad

REMOVAL:
1. Use a dull knife or spoon to remove as much as possible.

2. Rinse the back of the stain well with cold water.

3. Apply a laundry presoak (spot stain remover) and let stand several minutes.

4. Rub with a liquid enzyme detergent.

5. Launder according to garment label.

DAIRY PRODUCTS

BABY FORMULA

GENERAL
DESCRIPTION:
A special nutritive mixture, especially of milk or milk substitute with other ingredients in prescribed proportions, for feeding a baby. Formula was invented in 1867 by Henri Nestlé for mothers who were unable to breast-feed their babies. Since then, it has also become widely useful for children who are allergic to milk and milk products.

SEASON:
❄
Since a baby may rely on formula from birth well into the first year, a formula stain can appear in any season. Babies might spit up more during the winter months, if they experience those particularly dreadful infant colds, thus these stains could be more common in winter.

AREAS OF
OCCURRENCE:

This stain is undoubtedly most often found on the shoulders of all types of clothing. This includes both the front and the back of this part of a garment, as the most popular burping position for baby is over the shoulder. But babies are not choosy about where they spit up, so this stain may show up anywhere, from lapels to socks.

TIME OF
OCCURRENCE:
Any time you feed your baby is a time this stain can appear.

REMOVAL:
1. For fresh stains, soak and agitate the fabric thoroughly in cold water. For dried stains, soak fabric in a sudsy mixture of cold water and liquid enzyme detergent up to 30 minutes, until the stain is loosened.

2. Rinse well.

3. If the stain remains, rub a liquid enzyme detergent into the stain and let stand several minutes.

4. Launder according to garment label.

5. If the stain remains, make a paste of unseasoned meat tenderizer and water (at a ratio of approximately 3 to 1) and rub onto the stain.

6. Let paste dry, then brush it off and rinse the fabric well. If meat tenderizer is not available, soak the stain in enzyme detergent and cold water mixture for up to 30 minutes.

7. Apply a laundry presoak (spot stain remover) and launder again. On white fabrics, bleach any remaining stain by blotting with lemon juice and setting it to dry in the sunlight.

BUTTER OR MARGARINE

GENERAL DESCRIPTION:
BUTTER: **A fatty substance made by churning cream; used as a cooking medium, ingredient, and topping.** MARGARINE: **A butter substitute made from hydrogenized animal and/or vegetable fats.** Butter and margarine are ubiquitous—one or the other is used in just about every non-vegan prepared food on the market. They are also found all over the ingredient lists of most cookbooks in circulation.

SEASON:
Whether poured on popcorn, spread on holiday baked goods, or slathered on corn on the cob, butter and margarine cannot be escaped at any time of year.

	Butter and margarine are tricky, and can stain unsus-
AREAS OF OCCURRENCE:	pecting victims almost anywhere. Remember to get

AREAS OF OCCURRENCE: Butter and margarine are tricky, and can stain unsuspecting victims almost anywhere. Remember to get extra napkins at the movie theater, or the lap area of your pants will be in grave danger. Melted butter can also drip from popcorn, crab legs, baked potatoes, and corn on the cob.

VARIATIONS OF SIGNIFICANCE: Corn on the cob; popcorn; seafood; toast

REMOVAL: *On fabric:*

1. Use a dull knife or spoon to remove as much as possible.

2. Apply a laundry presoak (spot stain remover) and let stand for several minutes to allow it to penetrate fabric.

3. Rub liquid enzyme detergent into the stain and let stand several minutes.

4. Launder in the hottest water safe for the fabric.

On carpet:

1. Sprinkle with an absorbent powder such as baking soda or talcum powder. Let stand several hours.

2. Vacuum. Repeat until you have removed as much stain as possible.

3. If the stain remains, shampoo with a liquid carpet detergent according to manufacturer's directions. Or sprinkle with dry carpet-cleaning powder, let stand several hours, and then vacuum.

CHEESE

GENERAL DESCRIPTION: A dairy product made from the curds produced by coagulating milk using acid and enzymes. Common cheeses range from very firm (like an aged gouda) to soupy (like a cottage cheese). The variety of texture in cheese is rivaled only by the uses for it, which are countless. This calcium-rich food is also quite good for you (in moderation, as with all things). Cheese helps strengthen bones to prevent osteoporosis, and helps to prevent tooth decay. Firm cheeses, like cheddar, are most effective for these purposes. To receive the most beneficial results, eat cheese alone or just after a meal.

SEASON:

Comfort foods mainly consisting of melted cheeses, like lasagna and grilled cheese sandwiches, might be more common in winter. However, cheese is ever present at barbecues in the summer, so there may be no time of year you are safe from this stain.

AREAS OF OCCURRENCE:

Cheese is most likely to stain when melted—because of its consistency and tendency to plop in this state, laps of jeans and skirts are most susceptible. Stringy mozzarella can leave spots on the fronts and sleeves of turtlenecks and T-shirts alike. Given the popularity of omelets for breakfast, as well as grogginess in early morning, chef and diner can stain a nightgown or pair of pajamas with ease.

TIME OF OCCURRENCE: Late nights and early mornings are popular times to incur this stain, as defenses against it are down due to sleepiness.

Baked ziti; blintzes; burritos; cannoli; cheesecake;
cheesesteaks; enchiladas; grilled sandwiches; lasagna;
macaroni and cheese; manicotti; nacho dip; omelets;
pizza; quesadillas; quiche; soufflés; tacos

REMOVAL: *For fresh stains on fabric:*

1. Treat the stain as soon as possible. Soak and agitate fabric in cold water to loosen the stain, or sponge it with club soda.

2. If the stain remains, rub the stain with a liquid enzyme detergent and soak in tepid water for up to 30 minutes or until the stain is removed. Rub the stain lightly during soaking.

3. If the stain remains, apply a laundry presoak (spot stain remover) and let stand several minutes.

4. Launder according to garment label.

5. If a color stain remains, repeat steps 2 through 4.

For dried stains on fabric:

1. Use a dull knife or spoon to remove as much as possible.

2. Rub the stain with a liquid enzyme detergent and soak the garment in cold water for several hours or until the stain is removed. Rub the stain lightly during soaking.

3. See steps 3 through 5 for fresh stains.

ICE CREAM

<table>
<tr><td>GENERAL
DESCRIPTION:</td><td>A rich frozen dessert made with dairy products, sugar, eggs, and various flavorings. Because artificial cooling was such a luxury, ice cream spent a long time as a food for aristocracy only; the first public sales were at Café Procope, the first coffeehouse in Paris, in 1670. With the advancement of technology, ice cream has ranked among the favorite desserts of children and adults the world over. The ice cream stain is influenced by the ingredients that are added to it; therefore, some cross-referencing in this book may be necessary to effectively treat the stain at hand. (See Chocolate on page 73, Fruits or Berries on page 24.)</td></tr>
</table>

SEASON: Ice cream is a favorite summertime treat, so the probability of procuring this stain during the hottest months of the year is nearly one hundred percent. However, because ice cream is also a staple on many people's dessert and/or comfort-food menus, this stain occurs during any time of year.

AREAS OF OCCURRENCE: Ice-cream stains are nearly impossible to avoid due to the treat's ephemeral frozenness. The range of this stain is mind-boggling; ice cream can appear as far from the mouth as the socks or the shoes when walking while eating (especially due to faulty sugar-cone design). Be especially on guard against the "rolling stain," which occurs when a whole scoop of ice cream falls from the top of your cone and rolls down the entire length of the front of your shirt and/or shorts.

VARIATIONS OF SIGNIFICANCE:	Ice-cream cakes; milkshakes

REMOVAL: *For fresh stains on fabric:*

1.   Treat the stain as soon as possible. Soak and agitate fabric in cold water to loosen the stain, or sponge it with club soda.

2.   If the stain remains, rub it with a liquid enzyme detergent and soak in tepid water for up to 30 minutes or until the stain is removed. Rub the stain lightly during soaking.

3.   If the stain remains, apply a laundry presoak (spot stain remover) and let stand several minutes.

4.   Launder according to garment label.

5.   If a color stain remains, repeat steps 2 through 4.

6.   If a grease stain remains, place the stain facedown on an absorbent cloth and treat with dry-cleaning fluid according to manufacturer's directions.

For dried stains on fabric:

1.   Use a dull knife or spoon to remove as much as possible.

2.   Rub the stain with a liquid enzyme detergent and soak the garment in cold water for several hours or until the stain is removed. Occasionally rub the stain between your thumbs during soaking.

3.   See steps 3 through 6 for fresh stains, above.

MILK OR CREAM

GENERAL
DESCRIPTION:

MILK: **An opaque white liquid secreted by female mammals (in the context of human food, mostly cows) to nourish their young.** CREAM: **The fatty part of milk that rises to the surface before homogenization.** Despite the proliferation of excellent vegan alternatives, milk and cream still dominate dessert recipes and coffee preparations, and babies who aren't allergic live on the stuff. The low-fat craze of the 1990s temporarily knocked cream off its pedestal and made skim milk king (see Water Spots on page 156), but today's fad dieters may drink heavy cream as a treat.

SEASON:

Both coffee and baked goods are year-round goodies, and so milk or cream may find its way onto garments almost any time. The heavy baking months, during winter, are the most common times for this stain to occur.

AREAS OF
OCCURRENCE:

Since milk and cream are almost always found in liquid form—and when powdered, they won't likely stain—they tend to splash on sleeves and fronts of jackets and ties, especially in the early-morning rush to get coffee or cereal into your mouth. Additionally, since both of these dairy substances are highly spillable, shoes, socks, and pants are not immune to this stain.

TIME OF
OCCURRENCE:

Early morning is undoubtedly the time this stain is most often encountered. Since almost all breakfast foods include milk or cream, and given that breakfast is often a hurried affair, this is the time they will most frequently splash or drip onto your clothing.

VARIATIONS OF SIGNIFICANCE:	Cereal; coffee; cream soups; creamed vegetables; egg dishes; fettuccine Alfredo
REMOVAL:	*For fresh stains on fabric:*

1. Treat the stain as soon as possible. Soak and agitate fabric in cold water to loosen the stain, or sponge it with club soda.

2. If the stain remains, rub the stain with a liquid enzyme detergent and soak in tepid water for up to 30 minutes or until the stain is removed. Rub the stain lightly during soaking.

3. If the stain remains, apply a laundry presoak (spot stain remover) and let stand several minutes.

4. Launder according to garment label.

5. If a color stain remains, repeat steps 2 through 4.

For dried stains on fabric:

1. Use a dull knife or spoon to remove as much as possible.

2. Rub the stain with a liquid enzyme detergent and soak the garment in cold water for several hours or until the stain is removed. Occasionally rub the stain between your thumbs while soaking.

3. See steps 3 through 5 for fresh stains, above.

PUDDING

GENERAL DESCRIPTION: A soft, creamy, cooked dessert made with eggs, milk, sugar, and flavorings and thickened with flour or another starch. It is standard fare in the cafeterias of institutions like hospitals, schools, and nursing homes, as well as on the menus of diners and some restaurants (especially those with salad bars). It can be found in a wide variety of flavors; some favorites are tapioca, chocolate, vanilla, pistachio, and butterscotch. Pudding is often used as filling for pies, donuts, and other baked goods, and can even be frozen into ice pop form.

SEASON:

Most pudding is consumed when institutional cafeterias are at their peak of activity. Pudding is most prevalent during the school year, when school cafeterias strive to feed young minds.

AREAS OF OCCURRENCE: The items that pudding stains affect are influenced by the location in which the stain is acquired. If in a hospital, sheets, blankets, and hospital gowns are prime targets; if in a school cafeteria, the possibilities are endless due to the potential for food fights. In the case of a food fight, all articles of clothing are at risk, in every area.

TIME OF OCCURRENCE: Pay special attention during the hours of 11:00 a.m. to 1:00 p.m., as pudding is a dessert most often served with lunch.

VARIATIONS OF SIGNIFICANCE: Custards; pies; ice pops

REMOVAL: *For fresh stains on fabric:*

1. Treat the stain as soon as possible. Soak and agitate fabric in cold water to loosen the stain, or sponge it with club soda.

2. If the stain remains, rub the stain with a liquid enzyme detergent and soak in tepid water for up to 30 minutes or until the stain is removed. Rub the stain lightly during soaking.

3. If the stain remains, apply a laundry presoak (spot stain remover) and let stand several minutes.

4. Launder according to garment label.

5. If a color stain remains, repeat steps 2 through 4.

For dried stains on fabric:

1. Use a dull knife or spoon to remove as much as possible.

2. Rub the stain with a liquid enzyme detergent and soak the garment in cold water for several hours or until the stain is removed. Rub the stain lightly during soaking.

3. See steps 3 through 5 for fresh stains, above.

SOUR CREAM

GENERAL DESCRIPTION: Cream fermented with lactic acid bacteria. Sour cream is a true triple threat, being a major ingredient in many baked goods, a popular topping for savory recipes, and especially clutch in snacks (see: sour cream and onion dip). Sour cream is a popular accompaniment to spicy food; like other dairy products, it contains a protein that soothes taste buds.

SEASON:
☀ ❄

Summer is a popular time for favorites like tacos, nachos, and burritos. Since the baked potato is a favorite comfort food, winter months will see this stain as well.

AREAS OF
OCCURRENCE:

Sour cream is particularly plop prone; it can fall anywhere from the collar of your favorite shirt to the tips of your shoes.

VARIATIONS OF
SIGNIFICANCE:

Baked potatoes; burritos; chili; chip dips; nachos; quesadillas; tacos

REMOVAL:

For fresh stains on fabric:

1. Treat the stain as soon as possible. Soak and agitate fabric in cold water to loosen the stain, or sponge it with club soda.

2. If the stain remains, rub the stain with a liquid enzyme detergent and soak in tepid water for up to 30 minutes or until the stain is removed. Rub the stain lightly during soaking.

3. If the stain remains, apply a laundry presoak (spot stain remover) and let stand several minutes.

4. Launder according to garment label.

5. If a color stain remains, repeat steps 2 through 4.

For dried stains on fabric:

1. Use a dull knife or spoon to remove as much as possible.

2. Rub the stain with a liquid enzyme detergent and soak in cold water for several hours or until the stain is removed. Rub the stain lightly during soaking.

3. See steps 3 through 5 for fresh stains.

YOGURT

GENERAL DESCRIPTION: A thick, tart dairy product made from milk to which bacteria cultures have been added. Yogurt has achieved astounding popularity among the health-conscious. When Dannon started selling yogurt with strawberries at the bottom in 1947, Americans joined Europeans as fans of this now-ubiquitous food. Yogurt stains come in a variety of colors and consistencies, depending upon whether fruits or other flavorings have been added.

SEASON: Yogurt stains are evergreen, though there may be a notable increase in occurrence during the month of January, when millions of dieters are temporarily holding true to their New Year's resolution to eat healthier.

AREAS OF OCCURRENCE: Commonly seen on clothes associated with the gym or working out, yogurt stains are also found on the fronts of shirts and blouses, and the lap areas of pants.

TIME OF OCCURRENCE: Yogurt stains usually occur in early morning, lunchtime, and even in the late afternoon before dinner. Chances of a yogurt stain in the evening or late night are lower, but yogurt-based treats like lassi and frozen yogurt mean it's still possible.

VARIATIONS OF SIGNIFICANCE:	Frozen yogurt; yogurt-covered peanuts or raisins; yogurt drinks
REMOVAL:	*For fresh stains on fabric:*

1. Use a dull knife or spoon to remove as much as possible.

2. Rinse the back of the stain with cold water. Soak and agitate the fabric in cold water to loosen the stain, or sponge it with club soda.

3. If the stain remains, rub with a liquid enzyme detergent and soak in tepid water for up to 30 minutes or until it is removed. Rub the stain lightly during soaking.

4. If the stain remains, apply a laundry presoak (spot stain remover) and let stand several minutes.

5. Launder according to garment label.

6. If a color stain remains, repeat steps 2 through 5.

For dried stains on fabric:

1. Use a dull knife or spoon to remove as much as possible.

2. Rub the stain with a liquid enzyme detergent and soak the garment in cold water for several hours, or until the stain is removed. Occasionally rub the stain between your thumbs during soaking.

3. See steps 4 through 6 for fresh stains, above.

SAUCES *and* CONDIMENTS

BARBECUE OR STEAK SAUCES

GENERAL
DESCRIPTION:
Tangy sauces typically made of vinegar, tomatoes, sugar, and spices, used for basting meats, poultry, and vegetables to be cooked over an open flame or broiled. Barbecue or steak sauces can be brushed on food just before cooking or barbecuing, or can be used as marinades.

SEASON:
Barbecue sauce is most likely to stain clothing during the summer, when cookouts are par for the course. Steak sauce, however, can stain throughout the year, as both home cooking and fine dining involve T-bones or sirloins that may call for a little spicing up.

AREAS OF
OCCURRENCE:
Your "Kiss the Cook" apron is a prime candidate for a barbecue-sauce stain, since only a fool would cook on the grill without some protection. Bathing suits, shorts, and T-shirts are likely victims as well. Steak sauce could stain your gown, fur coat, or tuxedo, depending on the fanciness of your favorite restaurant, or the fare at a gala or benefit.

TIME OF
OCCURRENCE:
Summer barbecues are popular among family and friends. These can last well into the wee hours of the night. Any time from dusk until dawn is a fine time for a saucy stain of this sort.

REMOVAL:
1. Use a dull knife or spoon to remove as much as possible.

2. Flush the back of the stain immediately with cold water to force stain through the fabric.

3. Rub a liquid enzyme detergent into the stain and let stand several minutes. Occasionally rub the stain between your thumbs during soaking.

4. Rinse well.

△ 5. Sponge with a mild bleach, such as white vinegar, hydrogen peroxide, or lemon juice, then rinse well.

6. Repeat steps 3 through 4 until no more stain can be removed.

7. Apply a laundry presoak (spot stain remover) and let stand several minutes.

8. Launder with an enzyme detergent.

9. Let garment dry in the sun for added bleaching.

10. If the stain remains, rub an enzyme detergent into it and then soak the garment in warm water for up to 30 minutes or until the stain is removed.

11. Rinse well.

12. Apply laundry presoak (spot stain remover) and relaunder.

CARAMEL

GENERAL DESCRIPTION: A thick, golden to brown liquid produced by slowly heating white sugar until it reduces. Caramel is a popular flavoring for food of all kinds, including desserts, candies, and sweet and savory sauces. Although "butterscotch" and "caramel" are sometimes used interchangeably, butterscotch is made with brown sugar. Both are obtained by boiling sugar to or beyond 240 degrees Fahrenheit. Over the last decade, salted caramel has been the caramel of choice for many people, starting with an explosion in popularity in 2008. These days, the sweet-salty combo is no longer a craze, but it's still a popular flavor for higher-end treats like bonbons, gelato, and coffee drinks.

SEASON:

Caramel is a favorite of holiday bakers and ice-cream-sundae makers alike; therefore you are just as likely to run into this stain during the December holidays as in the heat of summer vacation. There is, however, always a chance of getting this stain when visiting the candy bar section at the local convenience store any time of year.

AREAS OF OCCURRENCE:

Caramel is a stringy substance, and it rarely stains as a single blob like most sauces and condiments do. This is a stain that might run from the front of your shirt to your arm, or vice versa.

TIME OF OCCURRENCE:
Caramel stains are most common after dinner and at Halloween, though caramel's presence in some fancy coffee drinks means you'll need to watch out in the morning as well.

VARIATIONS OF SIGNIFICANCE:
Candy bars; ice-cream sundaes

REMOVAL:
For fresh stains on fabric:

1. Use a dull knife or spoon to remove as much as possible.

2. Rinse well with cold water.

3. Rub liquid laundry detergent into the stain and let stand several minutes.

4. Rinse well in hot water, letting the water pass quickly through the fabric.

5. If the stain remains, stretch the stained fabric over a basin. Boil three or more cups of water in a pot or teakettle and pour over the stain from a height of 1 to 2 feet. (This may require two people: one to hold the fabric taut and the other to pour the water.) This procedure will force the stain through the fabric.

6. If the stain remains, apply a laundry presoak (spot stain remover) and launder according to garment label.

For dried stains on fabric:

1. Rub liquid laundry detergent into stain.

2. Soak garment in a soapy mixture of detergent and cold water for up to 30 minutes to loosen the stain. Agitate stain while soaking.

3. See steps 3 through 6 for fresh stains, above.

CHOCOLATE

GENERAL DESCRIPTION: A candy or beverage made from roasted and ground cacao seeds, generally sweetened. In its nearly three-thousand-year-old history, chocolate has been more than just a popular dessert or snack—it has served as medicinal tonic, religious symbol, currency, and even aphrodisiac. Today more than seven million tons of chocolate are consumed in the world each year. It is found in many forms, including powder, syrup, solid bars, molded woodland animals and popular cultural icons, and as flavoring for cakes, pastries, frostings, cookies, ice creams, puddings, custards, drinks, and other desserts, and even some hearty entrees, like chicken mole.

SEASON:

Chocolate stains can appear in any season but they are especially prevalent near holidays—particularly Christmas, Halloween, and Easter—as well as at times of celebration where dessert is likely to be served. Chocolate ice cream is almost certainly found more often on summer clothing, like tank tops and shorts, and cocoa is more prevalent during the cold winter months. There is an increased chance of chocolate stains during "break-up season," year-round.

AREAS OF OCCURRENCE:

Chocolate stains are found on the fronts of blouses and shirts, but aren't confined to those spots. Ice cream can travel as far as the pants, skirt, or shoes (see Ice Cream on page 59). Bakers, pastry chefs, waiters, and waitresses may run the risk of this stain every moment they're on the job.

TIME OF OCCURRENCE:

Chocolate stains will likely appear at dessert time. In some cases, they occur in the wee hours of a particularly trying night. You might not notice the stain at this time, as it would likely occur in a darkened room, with only the glow of the television as your light source.

VARIATIONS OF SIGNIFICANCE:

Chocolate chip cookies; chocolate-covered fruit; milkshakes; mole sauce

REMOVAL:	1.	Use a dull knife or spoon to remove as much as possible.
	2.	Rinse the back of the stain well with cold water.
	3.	Rub a liquid enzyme detergent into the stain, then soak it in cold water for 30 minutes or until the stain is loosened. Old, persistent stains may need to be soaked for several hours. Occasionally rub the stain between your thumbs as it soaks.
	4.	Rinse well and allow to dry.
	5.	If a grease stain remains, apply a laundry presoak (spot stain remover) or treat with dry-cleaning fluid according to manufacturer's directions.
	6.	Launder according to garment label.

GRAVY

GENERAL DESCRIPTION: The fat and juices of cooked foods, often diluted with water, milk, wine, or stock, and thickened with flour or cornstarch; used as a sauce. Gravy is generally known as a "reduction sauce," and can be made from the juices of many types of cooked food, from meat to vegetables. It's easy to make—though grocery stores generally carry it in cans—and complements a variety of recipes nicely. There is some controversy as to whether lumps are desirable in gravy; some say the lumps add a homemade flavor, others prefer their gravy smooth. Whichever way you have it, though, it will still stain linens and clothing.

SEASON: 	Turkey season is gravy-stain season; that is, Thanksgiving and Christmastime see more of these stains. Because a heaping plate of meat, potatoes, and vegetables smothered with gravy is a hearty and comforting meal, however, the occasional gravy stain may appear throughout winter and fall.
AREAS OF OCCURRENCE: 	Since gravy is a food with a tendency to splash and/or splatter, this is a far-reaching stain. The sleeves of a wool sweater or the lap areas of pants and skirts receive this stain the most. Tablecloths and napkins are especially vulnerable, as gravy boats are notoriously bad at containing all the drips.
TIME OF OCCURRENCE:	Dinnertime is the most common time to encounter this stain, though since some eat their big holiday meals early in the day, at a time considered lunchtime, and some eat later, there's no telling when you'll find it.
VARIATIONS OF SIGNIFICANCE:	Biscuits; chicken; french fries; pot roast; Salisbury steak; turkey
REMOVAL:	*On fabric:*

1. Use a dull knife or spoon to remove as much as possible.

2. Blot the stain with a paper towel.

3. Mix a solution of 1 tablespoon liquid enzyme detergent to 1 cup of cold water. Soak the fabric in the solution for several hours.

4. Rinse well.

5. If the stain persists, rub a liquid enzyme detergent into the stain.

6. Launder with liquid enzyme detergent.

7. If the stain remains, repeat steps 3 through 6.

On carpet:

1. Use a dull knife or spoon to remove as much as possible.

2. Blot remaining liquid with an absorbent cloth.

3. Sponge the stain with a sudsy mixture of liquid enzyme detergent and cold water, then sponge with clear cold water. Repeat until you have removed as much stain as possible.

4. If the stain remains, sponge with a mild bleach, such as lemon juice or hydrogen peroxide (do not let it saturate carpet), then sponge with clear cold water. Repeat as needed.

5. If the stain remains, treat with a carpet spotter according to manufacturer's directions.

HONEY

GENERAL DESCRIPTION: A sweet, syrupy liquid made by bees from flower nectar and stored in the cells of their hives for food; consumed fresh or after processing, it is usually used as a nutritive sweetener. Honey is not easily produced—bees must collect nectar from about two million flowers to make a one-pound comb of honey. However, once honey has been created, it's not easily gotten rid of. It seems it is the only food that does not spoil.

Honey found in the tombs of Egyptian pharaohs has proven to be edible, even after three thousand years.

SEASON:

❄

Honey is consumed year-round, but its stain is especially prevalent during the winter flu season, when honey-sweetened tea is just what the doctor orders.

AREAS OF OCCURRENCE:

Honey is a stringy substance, and it rarely stains as a single blob like most sauces and condiments do. Be alert for stringy and stretchy threads of honey that may affect multiple garments.

TIME OF OCCURRENCE:

Honey stains are most likely to appear in the morning, around breakfast, when an errant piece of honey-covered toast or biscuit escapes someone's grasp.

REMOVAL:

For fresh stains on fabric:

1. Use a dull knife or spoon to remove as much as possible.

2. Rinse well with cold water.

3. Rub liquid laundry detergent into the stain and let stand several minutes.

4. Rinse well in hot water, letting the water pass quickly through the fabric.

5. If the stain remains, stretch the stained fabric over a basin. Boil three or more cups of water in a pot or teakettle and pour over the stain from a height of 1 to 2 feet. (This may require two people: one to hold the fabric taut and the other to pour the water.) This procedure will force the stain through the fabric.

6. If the stain remains, apply a laundry presoak (spot stain remover) and launder according to garment label.

For dried stains on fabric:

1. Rub liquid laundry detergent into the stain. Soak the garment in a soapy mixture of detergent and cold water for up to 30 minutes to loosen the stain. Agitate stain while soaking.

2. See steps 3 through 6 for fresh stains, above.

KETCHUP

GENERAL DESCRIPTION:

A slightly sweet table condiment made with a base of pureed tomatoes, sugar, and vinegar. Older ketchup recipes used ingredients as varied as oysters, mushrooms, and fruit as a base, but the tomato has now achieved primacy, and virtually anyone who hears you say "ketchup" will assume you mean tomato ketchup. Primary uses for ketchup may vary from country to country: for example, in Scandinavia, on pasta; Eastern Europe, on pizza; Japan, on rice; Great Britain, on fish and chips; and in the United States, on hamburgers, hot dogs, and french fries.

SEASON:

While ketchup is inarguably the most popular condiment at a summer cookout, this won't be the only time and place you'll find this stain, since hamburgers and french fries are year-round foods. A ketchup stain could appear literally any time at all.

This is a foodstuff with a tendency to plop and splatter. From the collar of your windbreaker after eating a hot dog at the game, to the hem of your dress after the church picnic, ketchup is found to be an equal-opportunity stain.

REMOVAL:

1. Use a dull knife or spoon to remove as much as possible.

2. Flush the back of the stain immediately with cold water to force the stain through fabric.

3. Rub a liquid enzyme detergent into the stain and let stand several minutes. Rub the fabric between thumbs during soaking.

4. Rinse well.

5. Sponge with a mild bleach, such as white vinegar, hydrogen peroxide, or lemon juice, then rinse well.

6. Repeat steps 3 through 5 until no more stain can be removed.

7. Apply a laundry presoak (spot stain remover) and let stand several minutes.

8. Launder with an enzyme detergent.

9. Let garment dry in the sun for added bleaching.

10. If the stain remains, rub an enzyme detergent into the stain and then soak garment in warm water for up to 30 minutes or until the stain is removed. Rinse well.

11. Apply laundry presoak (spot stain remover) and relaunder.

MAPLE SYRUP

GENERAL DESCRIPTION: A sweet syrup made by reducing the sap of the North American maple tree. Between 30 and 50 gallons of maple sap are evaporated to yield one gallon of syrup, making the sugar content of syrup 66.5 percent, while the sugar content of the sap is only about 2.5 percent. In the United States, Vermont is the largest producer of this sticky substance, which is served as a sauce with pancakes, waffles, and other breakfast fare.

SEASON:

In the United States, mid-February through early April is considered "syrup season," the ideal time for harvesting maple sap—although climate change is pushing that season earlier. But the syrup that's produced and bottled during this period is a favorite at breakfast tables year-round, so this stain has potential unlimited by time.

AREAS OF OCCURRENCE: Maple-syrup stains appear most frequently on the fronts of shirts, blouses, jackets, and the lap areas of pants and dresses. Because maple syrup is most often consumed in the morning, as we struggle to regain our grasp of the world, pay close attention to the cuffs and elbows of sleeves; they are targets of this sticky stain when you are unaware.

TIME OF OCCURRENCE: Maple syrup stains aren't only acquired in the morning, though maple syrup is used to enhance the foods served at breakfast. With the rise of the 24-hour diner, truck drivers, folks working the third shift, and many teenagers consume pancakes with maple syrup at all hours.

REMOVAL: *On fabric:*

1.   Use a dull knife or spoon to remove as much as possible.

2.   Rinse well with cold water.

3.   Rub liquid laundry detergent into the stain. Let stand several minutes.

4.   Rinse well in hot water, letting the water pass quickly through the fabric.

5.   If the stain remains, stretch the stained fabric over a basin. Boil three or more cups of water in a pot or teakettle and pour over the stain from a height of 1 to 2 feet. (This may require two people: one to hold the fabric taut and the other to pour the water.) This procedure will force the stain through the fabric.

6.   If the stain remains, apply a laundry presoak (spot stain remover) and launder according to garment label.

MAYONNAISE

GENERAL DESCRIPTION: A creamy emulsified dressing made of egg yolks, vinegar or lemon juice, oil, and seasonings. The name mayonnaise (though not the idea of emulsifying egg yolks, or the idea of making a similar concoction) dates back to eighteenth century France. The Duke of Richelieu popularized the condiment after his victory over the British at the port of Mahon—hence, *mahonnaise*. (Where he got it from in the first place remains shrouded in legend; some stories even claim that he invented it.) This condiment has since become a staple in kitchens around the globe.

SEASON:

Though mayonnaise is probably more commonly used as a condiment for summer picnic foods, like potato salad and pasta salad, a large contingent of the population enjoys egg salad or tuna salad sandwiches throughout the year. Because of its wide appeal as an accompaniment to various foods, mayonnaise stains clothing year-round.

TIME OF OCCURRENCE:

You'll rarely find a need for mayonnaise in the morning. This stain appears most often at lunchtime, when a sandwich or french fries call for a healthy dollop of the stuff.

VARIATIONS OF SIGNIFICANCE:

Chicken salad; egg salad; ham salad; pasta salad; potato salad; sandwiches; tuna salad

REMOVAL:

On fabric:

1. Use a dull knife or spoon to remove as much as possible.

2. Apply a laundry presoak (spot stain remover). Let stand for several minutes.

3. Rub liquid enzyme detergent into the stain and let stand several minutes.

4. Launder in the hottest water safe for the fabric.

On carpet:

1. Sprinkle with an absorbent powder, such as baking soda or talcum powder. Let stand several hours.

2. Vacuum.

3. Repeat until you have removed as much stain as possible.

4. If the stain remains, shampoo with a liquid carpet detergent according to manufacturer's directions. Or sprinkle with dry carpet-cleaning powder, let stand several hours, and vacuum.

MUSTARD

GENERAL DESCRIPTION:
A smooth, somewhat runny condiment made from white, yellow, or brown mustard seeds, sugar, vinegar, and turmeric that has a mild, slightly sharp flavor and often a bright yellow color. Varieties of mustard include Chinese, English, German, and Dijon. It is standard fare on just about any fast-food hamburger or hot dog, as well as on many other popular snacks, such as soft pretzels. America's National Mustard Museum is located in Middleton, Wisconsin, and houses more than 5,000 mustard varieties (many of which are actually international).

SEASON:

Due to the ubiquitousness of fast food, mustard stains occur year-round. The popularity of backyard grills leads to an increase in the overall prevalence of mustard in spring and summer.

Mustard is a wily substance that will plop from unexpected places directly onto the fronts of shirts, pants, dresses, shorts, and skirts.

REMOVAL:

For fresh stains on fabric:

1. Use a dull knife or spoon to remove as much as possible.

2. Hold the stain upside down under a stream of cold water to force as much stain out of the fabric as possible.

3. Rub a liquid enzyme detergent into the stain (the stain may change color). Let stand for several minutes.

4. Rinse well. Repeat until no more stain can be removed.

5. Apply a laundry presoak (spot stain remover) and let stand several minutes.

6. Launder with a liquid enzyme detergent.

7. If the stain remains, let garment dry in the sun, then repeat steps 3 through 6.

For dried stains on fabric:

1. Rub glycerin into the stain and let stand until loosened, up to 1 hour.

2. See steps 2 through 6 for fresh stains, above.

On carpet:

1. For fresh stains, use a dull knife or spoon to remove as much as possible. If the stain is dry, first

rub glycerin into it and let stand until loosened, up to 1 hour, then scrape away as much as possible.

2. Blot the stain with a damp absorbent cloth.

3. If the stain remains, treat with a carpet spotter.

△ 4. Lighten any remaining color stain with a mild bleach, such as hydrogen peroxide, white vinegar, or lemon juice.

5. Blot with water.

OIL, COOKING OR VEGETABLE

GENERAL DESCRIPTION: Unctuous liquids (although some are solid at room temperature) used for cooking or flavoring food. The edible types of oils are made from such things as nuts, seeds, vegetables, legumes, and fruits. Though canola and vegetable oils are indispensable for everyday stovetop cooking, olive oil may have surpassed them in popularity, both for cooking and for flavoring. Historically, olive oil was used to light the candelabra in the ancient Temple of Jerusalem, as far back as 164 B.C. Today during Hanukkah, the finest olive oil is still used to light oil lamps and to cook traditional holiday foods.

SEASON: Since these oils are used to cook everything from popcorn to stir-fry, oil stains are not limited to or more common during any particular season, although the Hanukkah season does carry a slighty elevated risk of stains from sputtering oil used to fry latkes or sufganiyot.

Oil splatters easily; it pops and sputters when it gets hot. Therefore, no part of your clothing is safe from the stuff, though sleeves of sweaters and blouses, not to mention the fronts of aprons, are most vulnerable during cooking. Of course, when a food cooked in oil falls on your jeans or the front of your jacket, a stain will appear just as easily.

**VARIATIONS OF
SIGNIFICANCE:**

Chicken dishes; Chinese food; deep-fried foods; pasta dishes; pasta salad

REMOVAL:

On fabric:

1. Use a dull knife or spoon to remove as much as possible.

2. Apply a laundry presoak (spot stain remover), and let stand for several minutes.

3. If the stain remains, rub liquid enzyme detergent into the stain and let stand several minutes.

4. Launder in the hottest water safe for the fabric.

On wallpaper:

1. Use a dull knife or spoon to remove as much as possible.

2. Place a sheet of absorbent paper, such as a paper towel or brown paper bag (ink side up), over the stain and press with a warm iron. Replace the absorbent paper once saturated.

3. If the stain remains after pressing, make a paste of cornstarch or baking soda and water (at a ratio of approximately 3 to 1) and smear it on the stain.

4. Let the paste dry, then brush it off. Repeat as necessary.

5. Apply a laundry presoak (spot stain remover) and let stand several minutes.

6. Wipe off with a damp cloth.

7. Repeat as necessary.

On carpet:

1. Sprinkle with an absorbent powder, such as baking soda or talcum powder. Let stand several hours.

2. Vacuum. Repeat until you have removed as much stain as possible.

3. If the stain remains, shampoo with a liquid carpet detergent according to manufacturer's directions.

RELISH

GENERAL DESCRIPTION: A condiment made of cooked, pickled, or raw chopped vegetables or fruits; can be smooth or chunky, sweet or savory, and hot or mild. Relish is a standard condiment used at baseball parks, barbecues, and picnics—wherever there are grilled hot dogs, you are sure to find relish. According to the National Hot Dog and Sausage Council, chunky condiments like relish should be applied directly to the hot dog (not to the bun), just after wet condiments like mustard and chili but before spices, such as salt or pepper.

SEASON: Relish stains occur primarily in summertime but are known to occur even during the coldest days of winter at football stadiums across the United States.

AREAS OF OCCURRENCE: In summer, stains are likely to be found on T-shirts and shorts; in winter, on the fronts of brightly colored jackets bearing football team logos.

REMOVAL:

1. Rinse the back of the stain immediately and thoroughly with cold water to neutralize the acid.

2. Place garment on an absorbent cloth and sponge well with ammonia, starting from the outside of the stain's edge. Replace cloth underneath as it becomes saturated. (If treating stains on wool or silk, dilute ammonia with an equal amount of cold water.) If ammonia is not available, substitute a baking-soda paste by mixing baking soda with water at a ratio of approximately 3 to 1. Rub paste into stain.

3. Rinse well.

4. Repeat as needed.

5. If a color stain remains, apply a laundry presoak (spot stain remover) and let stand several minutes.

6. Launder according to garment label.

SALAD DRESSING, CREAMY

GENERAL DESCRIPTION: A sauce used on any type of salad, made from a base of mayonnaise, yogurt, sour cream, or buttermilk with spices or vegetables added for flavor. French and Russian salad dressings do not come from France and

Russia. Although Russian dressing once contained a Russian ingredient (caviar), they both remain purely American concoctions. Other popular varieties at salad bars include ranch, bleu cheese, and Parmesan.

SEASON:

Even though salads themselves are probably most popular during the summer months, creamy salad dressings are often used in baked dishes throughout the year, so their stains aren't limited to the warmest time of the year.

AREAS OF OCCURRENCE:

This thick, liquidy substance tends to land on clothing in the lap areas, as well as on sleeves and fronts of garments.

TIME OF OCCURRENCE:

Since salad dressing is primarily used to enhance salad, and salad is primarily served as a complete lunch or a side dish with dinner, afternoons and evenings are when you'll be most likely to encounter this stain.

VARIATIONS OF SIGNIFICANCE:

Baked ranch chicken; pasta dishes; salad; vegetable dip

REMOVAL:

1. Use a dull knife or spoon to remove as much as possible.

2. Rub the stain with a liquid enzyme detergent and soak in cold water for up to 30 minutes or until the stain is removed. Rub the stain lightly between thumbs during soaking.

3. If the stain remains, apply a laundry presoak (spot stain remover) and let stand several minutes.

4. Launder according to garment label.

5. If a color stain remains, repeat steps 2 through 4.

SALAD DRESSING, VINAIGRETTE

GENERAL
DESCRIPTION:
An emulsion of oil and vinegar (usually three parts oil and one part vinegar) seasoned with herbs, spices, salt, and pepper. Known to some as Italian dressing and to others as French, vinaigrette is quite possibly the most popular salad dressing in Western cultures. This dressing's stains are difficult to treat due to the difference in the consistency and makeup of the two main ingredients, oil and vinegar. (See Vinegar on page 97; Oil, Cooking or Vegetable on page 86.)

SEASON:

Vinaigrette stains are not particular to a season, though they may be more prevalent in warmer months when light lunches of lettuce and pasta salads are standard fare.

AREAS OF
OCCURRENCE:

A stray vinaigrette-covered vegetable from a salad or sandwich has a standard downward trajectory and therefore, vinaigrette stains are most common on the fronts of shirts, blouses, and jackets, and on the lap areas of pants and dresses. Before shaking a bottle of vinaigrette, always be sure to check that the cap is tightly secured, or you may find yourself with stains anywhere on your body or anywhere in the room (especially on the walls).

REMOVAL:

1. Use a dull knife or spoon to remove as much as possible.

2. Apply a laundry presoak (spot stain remover) and let stand several minutes to allow it to penetrate fabric.

3. Rub liquid enzyme detergent into the stain and let stand several minutes.

4. Launder in the hottest water safe for the fabric.

On wallpaper or walls:

1. Make a paste of cornstarch or baking soda and water at a ratio of approximately 3 to 1, then smear the paste onto stain. Non-gel toothpaste can also be used. Let paste dry, then wipe with a clean cloth. For toothpaste, let stand 10 to 15 minutes, then wipe with a damp cloth.

2. Repeat until the stain is gone.

SALSA

GENERAL DESCRIPTION: Literally the Spanish word for "sauce," a cooked or fresh combination of fruits and/or vegetables. The most common salsa is the refreshing mixture of tomatoes and chili peppers. Salsa has enjoyed an amazing rise in popularity in recent years due to its versatility and healthfulness; it goes with much more than just Mexican fare, and is generally fat-free.

SEASON: Due to the popularity of Mexican food in general and salsa in particular, you may encounter salsa stains throughout the year.

AREAS OF OCCURRENCE: Since margaritas often accompany Mexican dinners, there is virtually no limit to where you'll find salsa stains on clothing. Additionally, since salsa comprises both liquid and solid matter, it will run as well as plop, thus the fronts of dresses, trousers, and jackets are not safe from the salsa stain.

TIME OF OCCURRENCE:	Salsa may show up in breakfast foods, such as omelets; therefore, you might encounter this stain in the morning, though that will not be the norm. Afternoons and evenings are the times you are most likely to acquire this stain, though the amount of tequila you imbibe during the consumption of salsa could impair the process of detection until the next day or later.
VARIATIONS OF SIGNIFICANCE:	Mexican dishes; omelets

REMOVAL:

1. Use a dull knife or spoon to remove as much as possible.

2. Flush the back of the stain immediately with cold water to force the stain through fabric.

3. Rub a liquid enzyme detergent into the stain and let stand several minutes. Occasionally rub the stain between your thumbs during soaking.

4. Rinse well.

5. Sponge with a mild bleach, such as white vinegar, hydrogen peroxide, or lemon juice, then rinse well.

6. Repeat steps 3 through 5 until no more stain can be removed.

7. Apply a laundry presoak (spot stain remover) and let stand several minutes.

8. Launder with an enzyme detergent. Let garment dry in the sun for added bleaching.

9. If the stain remains, rub an enzyme detergent into the stain and then soak garment in warm water for up to 30 minutes or until the stain is gone.

10. Rinse well.

11. Apply laundry presoak (spot stain remover) and relaunder.

SOY SAUCE

GENERAL DESCRIPTION: A sauce made from fermented boiled soybeans and roasted wheat or barley; its color ranges from light to dark brown and its flavor is generally rich and salty. Soy sauce is a staple condiment of Asian cuisine. It can be found in many forms, including small packages with Chinese or Japanese take-out, in little pitchers on the tables of Chinese and Japanese restaurants, or in bottles for sale at supermarkets.

AREAS OF OCCURRENCE: Soy sauce stains are difficult to avoid when opening those small packets that are included with Chinese or Japanese take-out. Even when opened with extreme care, these little packets often spray all over the place, staining not only the sleeves and fronts of blouses, shirts, and dresses but trousers, shorts, skirts, and tablecloths, upholstered furniture, rugs, and carpets. These areas can also be affected when a novice attempts to use chopsticks. An errant dumpling will inevitably land in the dish of soy sauce, splattering the contents.

TIME OF OCCURRENCE: Soy sauce stains typically occur at times outside of common mealtimes, such as when you are running behind schedule and want a quick bite to eat before an engagement to which it is important to be punctual.

REMOVAL: *For fresh stains on fabric:*

1. Force cold water through the back of the stain.

2. Rinse well.

3. If the stain remains, apply a laundry presoak (spot stain remover) and let stand several minutes.

4. Launder according to garment label.

For dried stains on fabric:

1. Force cold water through the back of the stain.

2. Rinse well.

3. Rub liquid laundry detergent into the stain and let stand several minutes. Rub the stain between your thumbs as you rinse it in cold water. Repeat until you have removed as much stain as possible.

4. If the stain remains, rub with liquid laundry detergent and soak in lukewarm water, agitating often, for up to 30 minutes or until the stain is removed.

5. Rinse well.

6. See steps 3 and 4 for fresh stains, above.

TOMATO SAUCE

GENERAL DESCRIPTION: A mixture of tomatoes, vegetables, and spices, pureed or stirred together to make a sauce that can be thin or chunky in consistency and that is used to accent pastas and a variety of other foods. Though tomato sauce may seem quintessentially Italian, tomatoes were actually introduced to Italy from the Americas.

SEASON: Since there are so many different varieties of tomato sauce, and since the uses for tomato sauce are so diverse, stains from the stuff know no season.

AREAS OF OCCURRENCE: Your apron and sleeves will bear the brunt of this stain as you concoct your favorite tomato sauce, since it tends to pop and sputter as it simmers. While eating the delicious mixture, you'll find that no matter how thick or chunky with vegetables it is, it is a liquid that will splatter quite easily, so watch pant legs, collars, and sweaters for telltale signs of the Italian meal well-enjoyed.

TIME OF OCCURRENCE: Evening will most certainly be the time when this stain occurs (unless you are having shakshuka for breakfast). The dimness of most good Italian restaurants and the copious red wine that accompanies Italian meals might make detection an event for the next day. (See Wine, Red on page 116.)

VARIATIONS OF SIGNIFICANCE: Eggplant, chicken, or veal Parmesan; lasagna; manicotti; pizza; spaghetti

REMOVAL: 1. Use a dull knife or spoon to remove as much as possible.

2. Flush the back of the stain immediately with cold water to force the stain through fabric.

3. Rub a liquid enzyme detergent into the stain and let stand several minutes. Rub the fabric between thumbs.

4. Rinse well.

⚠ 5. Sponge with a mild bleach, such as white vinegar, hydrogen peroxide, or lemon juice, then rinse well.

6. Repeat steps 3 through 5 until no more stain can be removed.

7. Apply a laundry presoak (spot stain remover) and let stand several minutes.

8. Launder with an enzyme detergent.

9. Let garment dry in the sun for added bleaching.

10. If the stain remains, rub an enzyme detergent into the stain and then soak garment in warm water for up to 30 minutes or until the stain is gone.

11. Rinse well.

12. Apply laundry presoak (spot stain remover) and relaunder.

VINEGAR

GENERAL DESCRIPTION: From the French *vin aigre* (sour wine), a weak solution of acetic acid made from a fermented liquid such as cider, wine, champagne, or beer, subjected to certain bacterial activity. It is generally clear, but may be slightly tinted. Vinegar was the most potent acid known to the ancients; Pliny described Cleopatra dissolving a pearl in vinegar and then drinking the concoction (this probably wouldn't work, but try it if you have extra pearls). It is now most likely found as an ingredient in marinades or salad dressings, though it can also accompany salty foods like potato chips and french fries. In the United Kingdom, malt vinegar is the traditional condiment for fish and chips, although in 2016 there was a minor scandal when it was discovered that many fish and chip shops were using an ersatz malt vinegar substitute.

SEASON:

Vinegar stains occur at all times of year. However, you must have a heightened awareness of the potential for vinegar stains during spring, summer, and early fall, when vendors at fairs, amusement parks, and ball parks sell french fries seasoned with vinegar in leaky paper cups and cones.

AREAS OF OCCURRENCE:

This stain is most likely to be found on the fronts of jeans, shorts, blouses, dresses, jackets, and sweaters, but can sometimes reach as far as your shoes when vinegar is used as a condiment for french fries. When using vinegar to clean windows, be extra careful of sleeves.

TIME OF OCCURRENCE:

The acidity of vinegar makes it an unlikely choice in breakfast foods, thus, vinegar stainings are most likely during the salad course of midday or evening meals or times of recreation.

VARIATIONS OF SIGNIFICANCE:

Condiment for french fries; glass cleaner; marinades for meat; vinaigrette

REMOVAL:

1. Rinse the back of the stain immediately and thoroughly with cold water to neutralize the acid.

2. Place garment on an absorbent cloth and sponge well with ammonia, starting from the outside of the stain's edge. Replace the cloth underneath as it becomes saturated. (If treating stains on wool or silk, dilute ammonia with an equal amount of cold water.) If ammonia is not available, substitute a baking-soda paste, mixing baking soda and water at a ratio of approximately 3 to 1. Rub into stain.

3. Rinse well.

4. Repeat as needed.

5. If a color stain remains, apply a laundry presoak (spot stain remover) and let stand several minutes.

6. Launder according to garment label.

WORCESTERSHIRE SAUCE

GENERAL DESCRIPTION: A dark, spicy condiment usually made of soy sauce, vinegar, garlic, tamarind, onions, molasses, lime, anchovies, and other seasonings, originally bottled in Worcestershire, England. Though not as popular as its close cousin soy sauce, it is instrumental in seasoning foods, from meat, gravy, and soup to snack mixes and Bloody Marys. Testifying to its quiet but enduring popularity, Worcestershire sauce has been commercially available for more than 180 years.

SEASON: Because the sauce is most frequently used in heavier fare, such as meat, gravy, and hearty soups, a Worcestershire stain will most probably occur more in the colder months of the year.

AREAS OF
OCCURRENCE:
Another of those liquid condiments that splatter easily, especially because of the bottle it so often comes in; this sauce will splash onto cuffs and collars, as well as the fronts of blouses and slacks.

TIME OF
OCCURRENCE:
This stain will most likely strike in the hours between dusk and dawn, the most popular time for Worcestershire-friendly meals such as steak and burgers. One important exception, though, is the Bloody Mary, beloved as a brunch cocktail (especially among those nursing a hangover from the night before). For morning Worcestershire stains, you may also want to see Tomato Juice on page 114 and Liquor on page 104.

VARIATIONS OF
SIGNIFICANCE:
Barbecue sauce; Bloody Mary; gravy; marinades; snack mixes; soups

REMOVAL:

1. Rinse the back of the stain immediately and thoroughly with cold water to neutralize the acid.

2. Place the garment on an absorbent cloth and sponge well with ammonia, starting from the outside of the stain's edge. Replace the cloth underneath as it becomes saturated. (If treating stains on wool or silk, dilute ammonia with an equal amount of cold water.) If ammonia is not available, substitute a baking-soda paste, mixing baking soda and water at the ratio of approximately 3 to 1. Rub paste into stain.

3. Rinse well.

4. Repeat as needed.

5. If a color stain remains, apply a laundry presoak (spot stain remover) and let stand several minutes.

6. Launder according to garment label.

BEVERAGES

LIQUOR AND MIXED DRINKS

GENERAL DESCRIPTION: Any of a large number of drinks that contain a distilled alcoholic mixture of some kind, including vodka, gin, whiskey, and scotch, among others. Can be combined with other potables (such as tonic water, juices, colas, or another alcoholic mixture), or served alone, with or without ice. It is not uncommon to hear someone claim alcohol played an integral part in their marital status, financial affairs, or conception.

SEASON:

Alcoholic beverages often figure prominently in both times of celebration and times of trauma; thus their stains occur throughout the year. Many holidays and vacations involve consumption of alcohol, and these beverages often play a role in human mating rituals.

AREAS OF OCCURRENCE:

These stains may appear anywhere on the fronts of shirts and dresses, or may be splashed on pant legs and skirts as the hours grow later. The eventuality that another person might accidentally knock their glass into your back makes for stains that are noticeable to all but yourself.

TIME OF OCCURRENCE: Stainings are most likely during the evening and late-night hours, when parties, celebrations, and bar happenings take place. Although brunch drinks are a time-honored tradition, you are unlikely to be stained by an alcoholic beverage before 10 a.m. You are, however, apt to find a stain in the morning when reviewing the previous night's activities.

REMOVAL:
1. Rinse the back of stain well with cold water or club soda.

2. If the stain remains, rub with dishwashing liquid or liquid enzyme detergent. Let stand several minutes. (Do not use bar or natural soap of any kind or the stain will set.)

3. Rinse well with cold water.

4. Launder according to garment label.

5. If the stain remains, rub it with liquid enzyme detergent, then soak and agitate in cold water for 30 minutes or until the stain is removed.

6. Rinse well.

7. Apply laundry presoak (spot stain remover) and let stand several minutes.

8. Launder according to garment label.

BEER

GENERAL DESCRIPTION:
A beverage brewed from fermented grains (usually malted barley), flavored with hops. Beer is one of the most popular alcoholic beverages in the U.S., Canada, Great Britain, Ireland, and Germany. In Ireland around 70 percent of the barley crop goes to the production of Guinness, Ireland's most popular brew.

SEASON:

Beer is certainly a year-round drink, though different types are popular at different times of the year. Lighter beer, like pilsner and lager, is more popular in the summer, when the heat makes for extreme thirst; darker, heavier beer, like stout and porter, is more popular in the winter. This means that beer stains will likely appear throughout the year, though the color of the stains will vary.

Spilled beer is an epidemic in bars across the land, which means that no part of your clothing is safe, from the seat of your jeans to the back of your jacket. Depending on the type of drinking game you play, you could even encounter beer stains in such out-of-the-way spots as underthings and socks.

TIME OF
OCCURRENCE:

The hours between dusk and dawn are probably the most likely for you to experience a stain from beer, though it might not become apparent until the next day, when your vision may be clearer.

REMOVAL:

1. Rinse well.

2. Mix 1 teaspoon of a liquid enzyme detergent or dishwashing liquid with 1 cup of lukewarm water. (Do not use bar or natural soap of any kind on the fabric or the stain will set.) Pour mixture on stain and blot with an absorbent cloth. Replace the cloth as it becomes saturated.

3. Rinse well.

4. Make a mixture of 2 parts water to 1 part vinegar. Pour mixture on stain and blot quickly. Do not let the mixture sit on the fabric, since vinegar is a mild bleach.

5. Rinse well in warm water.

6. Launder according to garment label.

COFFEE

GENERAL DESCRIPTION: A drink made from the roasted and ground seeds of several trees or shrubs in the genus *Coffea*, percolated or infused in water. Coffee has earned a special place among favorite beverages worldwide, due in large part to its chemical makeup. Coffee contains a high percentage of caffeine, a substance that can help enforce alertness. At up to $600 (U.S.) a pound, kopi luwak coffee, grown in Indonesia, ranks as the most expensive coffee in the world.

SEASON: Coffee stains transcend season, as coffee is available year-round and many people swear by it as the only remedy for morning or afternoon sleepiness.

AREAS OF OCCURRENCE: Though it is a dangerous undertaking, many commuters hold cups or mugs of coffee between their legs as they ride or drive to work in the morning, making stains in this area especially likely. Other areas where stains are often found include furniture, jackets, coats, and the fronts of garments worn on the top of the body. Those who wear neckties may find that these seem to seek out open cups of coffee, so that the tips are often at risk for stains.

TIME OF OCCURRENCE: Hot coffee is an essential part of the morning ritual for many people, but some folks are so addicted to coffee that they'll continue to drink it all day and into the night. Many teenagers and college students drink coffee into the wee hours of the morning at "bottomless cup" diners and all-night restaurants—sometimes to stay awake to study, sometimes as a lubricant for conversation.

VARIATIONS OF SIGNIFICANCE:	Café au lait; cappuccino; chocolate-covered beans; coffee-flavored ice cream; latte
REMOVAL:	*On fabric:*

◐ 1. Rinse back of stain well with cold water until you've removed as much stain as possible.

2. Rub a liquid enzyme detergent into the remaining stain and let stand several minutes. For old or dried stains, rub the stain with detergent, then soak the garment in cold water for up to 30 minutes or until the stain is loosened.

⎍ 3. Launder with an enzyme detergent.

4. If the stain remains, rub it again with the enzyme detergent and soak garment in warm water for 10 to 15 minutes, then rinse well.

🗴 5. Apply a laundry presoak (spot stain remover) and let stand several minutes.

or

Make a paste of borax and water at a ratio of approximately 3 to 1 and spread it on the stain. Let stand 30 minutes, then brush off. Repeat until you have removed as much stain as possible.

⎍ 6. Relaunder with enzyme detergent.

On carpet:

1. Blot as much liquid out of the carpet as possible.

2. Saturate stain with club soda or cold water, then blot again.

3. Apply a carpet spotter according to manufacturer's directions.

or

Spread non-gel shaving cream onto the stain and work into the carpet with an old toothbrush. Rinse with cold water or club soda, then blot.

or

 Mix borax with warm water to make a paste at a ratio of approximately 3 to 1 and rub into stain. Let paste dry, then vacuum. Rinse with cold water or club soda, then blot.

 4. If the stain remains, sponge with a mild bleach, such as white vinegar or hydrogen peroxide. Let stand 15 minutes.

5. Blot.

6. Sponge well with water or club soda and blot with a dry cloth.

SOFT DRINKS

GENERAL DESCRIPTION: Non-alcoholic beverages that are usually carbonated, such as root beer, cola, or ginger ale. Coca-Cola is the most popular soft drink in the world, but when originally invented it contained both alcohol and coca, the plant that produces cocaine, and was marketed as a medicinal nerve tonic. After Prohibition, it rebranded as a "temperance drink" for those avoiding alcohol (still a major use of soft drinks today). It was still promoted as a medicine for complaints ranging from indigestion to impotence (not a major use of soft drinks today).

SEASON: Stains from soft drinks are a year-round concern. Though cold beverages are often considered a summer drink, true soda addicts don't take a break just because it's chilly out.

AREAS OF OCCURRENCE: Because sodas are carbonated and their bottles are tightly sealed, the probability that the pressure will build up and make them spray when opened is high; when this happens, all areas of clothing, furniture, walls, and flooring may fall victim to this stain.

TIME OF OCCURRENCE: Die-hard soda drinkers may obtain this stain in the morning, but staining will usually occur in the afternoon or evening, when this beverage is most often consumed.

VARIATIONS OF SIGNIFICANCE: Mixed drinks; punch

REMOVAL: *For fresh stains on fabric:*

1. Blot immediately with an absorbent cloth. Absorb as much liquid as possible.

2. Sponge or soak the stain with cold water.

3. Rub liquid enzyme detergent into stain. Let stand several minutes.

4. Launder in the hottest water safe for the fabric.

5. If the stain remains, apply a laundry presoak (spot stain remover), then launder, adding a bleach that is safe for the fabric. Test first for colorfastness.

For dried stains on fabric:

1. Soften the stain by rubbing glycerin into the cloth.

2. Let stand for 30 minutes. If glycerin is not available, soak the stain in a sudsy liquid enzyme detergent mixture until the stain is loosened.

3. Rinse well in cold water.

4. Follow steps 3 through 5 for fresh stains, above.

On carpet:

1. Blot immediately with an absorbent cloth. Absorb as much liquid as possible.

2. Sponge with a sudsy mixture of liquid laundry detergent and cold water. Continue until you have removed as much stain as possible.

3. Sponge with a clean, damp cloth, then let dry.

4. Vacuum.

5. If the stain remains, repeat steps 2 through 4 as needed.

6. If the stain remains, apply a carpet spotter according to manufacturer's directions.

TEA

<table>
<tr><td>GENERAL
DESCRIPTION:</td><td>An aromatic beverage prepared from the dried leaves, leaf buds, and internodes of the tea bush, infused in boiling water. Tea can also be made from a number of other herbs—it is then called "herbal tea." Chinese and Japanese cultures have elaborate ceremonies, created thousands of years ago, that cover the serving and consumption of tea. Though Britain may be the country most associated with tea-drinking as a hobby, its actual per-capita tea consumption lags behind both Ireland and Turkey.</td></tr>
<tr><td>SEASON:
☼ ❄</td><td>Tea is consumed year-round, and stains therefore may be attained at any time. Hot tea is popular during the colder months, while iced tea is a standard beverage during summer. There is an increase in tea drinking (and in turn, staining) during cold and flu season, when doctors recommend drinking tea with lemon to aid in respiration and to ward off fever.</td></tr>
<tr><td>AREAS OF
OCCURRENCE:
</td><td>Tea stains are often found on furniture, jackets, coats, dressing gowns, the lap areas of pants, and on the fronts of garments worn on the top of the body. The fronts and cuffs of clean, starched white shirts are particularly at risk, as well as the tips of neckties, which seem to seek out open cups.</td></tr>
<tr><td>TIME OF
OCCURRENCE:</td><td>Tea stains can be found morning, noon, and night. Some herbal varieties are popular at night before bedtime, and at this sleepy hour you must be particularly vigilant against staining.</td></tr>
</table>

REMOVAL: *On fabric:*

1. Rinse back of stain well with cold water until you've removed as much as possible.

2. Rub a liquid enzyme detergent into the remaining stain and let stand several minutes. For old or dried stains, rub the stain with detergent, then soak the garment in cold water for up to 30 minutes or until the stain is loosened.

3. Launder with an enzyme detergent.

4. If the stain remains, rub the stain again with the enzyme detergent, soak garment in warm water for 10 to 15 minutes.

5. Rinse well.

6. Apply a laundry presoak (spot stain remover) and let stand several minutes.

or

Make a paste of borax and water at a ratio of approximately 3 to 1 and spread it onto the stain. Let stand 30 minutes, then brush off. Repeat until you have removed as much stain as possible.

7. Relaunder with enzyme detergent.

On carpet:

1. Blot as much liquid out of the carpet as possible.

2. Saturate stain with club soda or cold water, then blot again.

3. Apply a carpet spotter according to manufacturer's directions.

or

Spread non-gel shaving cream onto the stain and work into the carpet with an old toothbrush. Rinse with cold water or club soda, then blot.

or

 Mix borax with warm water to make a paste at a ratio of approximately 3 to 1 and rub into stain. Let paste dry, then vacuum. Rinse with cold water or club soda, then blot.

 4. If the stain remains, sponge with a mild bleach, such as white vinegar or hydrogen peroxide. Let stand 15 minutes.

5. Blot with a dry cloth.

6. Sponge well with water or club soda, then blot.

TOMATO JUICE

GENERAL DESCRIPTION: The thick liquid that comes from squeezing the mildly acidic pulpy berry known as a tomato, drunk as juice. Popular as both a healthy breakfast drink and a mixer used with alcohol, tomato juice is also the official state beverage of Ohio. Though its primary use is as a drink, tomato juice is also useful for getting smells off pets—if a dog is sprayed by a skunk, the sure cure is a bath in tomato juice.

| SEASON: | Tomato juice is popular at breakfast tables and in Bloody Marys year round, and its stains won't be confined to a particular season. |

SEASON: Tomato juice is popular at breakfast tables and in Bloody Marys year round, and its stains won't be confined to a particular season.

AREAS OF OCCURRENCE: The lap areas of pants, skirts, and shorts are prime for this stain, which is thick, though also runny. Other areas that might fall victim to this stain are cuffs of blouses and jackets, as well as nightgowns and pajamas.

REMOVAL:

1. Use a dull knife or spoon to remove as much as possible.

2. Flush the back of the stain immediately with cold water to force stain through fabric.

3. Rub a liquid enzyme detergent into the stain and let stand several minutes. Rub the fabric between thumbs, then rinse well.

4. Sponge with a mild bleach, such as white vinegar, hydrogen peroxide, or lemon juice, then rinse well.

5. Repeat steps 3 and 4 until no more stain can be removed.

6. Apply a laundry presoak (spot stain remover) and let stand several minutes.

7. Launder with an enzyme detergent.

8. Let garment dry in the sun for added bleaching.

9. If the stain remains, rub an enzyme detergent into the stain and then soak garment in warm water for up to 30 minutes or until the stain is gone.

10. Rinse well.

11. Apply laundry presoak (spot stain remover) and relaunder.

WINE, RED

GENERAL
DESCRIPTION:

A fermented juice made from black grapes, which derives its color from the contact between the juice and the grape skins during fermentation; the colors range from pink to dark red. The strong, bold flavors of red wine produce equally strong, tricky stains. True partiers and bon vivants should remember that one of the best ways to remove a red wine stain is dousing the area with white wine.

SEASON:

Though red wine is served year-round, most people prefer to drink the heartier red wines in fall and winter. Stains are often found on the formal attire of those attending holiday parties, and on the carpets and rugs of those hosting these holiday gatherings.

AREAS OF
OCCURRENCE:

Staining may be anywhere on the fronts of shirts and dresses, as well as splashed on pant legs and skirts as the hours grow later. You must allow for the eventuality that someone at your party will place their glass on the floor next to their chair and promptly kick it over, spilling the glass's contents onto the floor. Another common spot for occurrence are the altar garments and clothes worn by Communion participants at Catholic masses.

TIME OF
OCCURRENCE:

During a particularly engaging dinner party or gathering of friends, red wine stains may not be detected until later in the evening, or even the next morning, depending upon the amount consumed.

VARIATIONS OF SIGNIFICANCE: Coq au vin; beef bourguignon; pasta sauces; red-wine vinaigrettes; sangria

REMOVAL: *On fabric:*

1. Pour white wine, club soda, or cold water on the stain immediately.

2. Blot with an absorbent cloth, then sprinkle salt onto the stain and let stand 1 to 2 minutes.

3. Rinse in cold water and rub out the stain.

4. If the stain remains, repeat steps 1 through 3 until no more stain can be removed.

5. Rub a liquid enzyme detergent into the stain and let stand several minutes.

6. Rinse with cold water.

7. If the stain remains, apply a laundry presoak (spot stain remover).

8. Launder with a liquid enzyme detergent.

On carpet:

1. Blot up as much wine as possible with an absorbent cloth.

2. Saturate the stain with club soda or cold water.

3. Repeat steps 1 and 2 as needed.

4. If stain remains, make a paste of borax or baking soda and water at a ratio of approximately 3 to 1.

Smear paste onto stain with an old toothbrush and let dry.

 5. Vacuum.

6. Repeat until no more stain can be removed.

7. If the stain remains, treat with a carpet spotter.

WINE, WHITE

GENERAL
DESCRIPTION:

A fermented juice made from white (and occasionally, red) grapes; because there is minimal, if any, contact between the juice and the skins during fermentation, its color can vary from pale to almost amber. White wine is often best served chilled, but only for about two hours—refrigerating white wine or champagne for more than a few hours can dull both the flavor and the bouquet.

SEASON:

White wine is best drunk with light fare, such as poultry and fish, and dishes that are most popular during the summer months. Champagne is the customary drink at any big celebration, especially New Year's Eve, but since the good times aren't limited by season, neither is the potential for a white wine stain.

AREAS OF
OCCURRENCE:

This stain is found anywhere on the fronts of shirts and dresses, as well as splashed on pant legs and skirts. Be alert to the possibility of another person accidentally knocking their glass into your back, causing stains that are difficult to detect.

TIME OF
OCCURRENCE:

White wine stains are most likely to be achieved during the evening and late-night hours, when parties, celebrations, and bars are often visited. You are unlikely to obtain a stain from white wine before 10 a.m., with the exception of an occasional mimosa (in which the orange juice is the likely culprit anyway).

VARIATIONS OF SIGNIFICANCE: Champagne; champagne cocktails; marinades and sauces; some sangrias; white-wine vinegar

REMOVAL:

1. Rinse back of stain well with cold water or club soda.

 2. If the stain remains, rub with dishwashing liquid or liquid enzyme detergent. Let stand several minutes. (Do not use bar or natural soap of any kind or the stain will set.)

 3. Rinse well with cold water.

4. Launder according to garment label.

5. If the stain remains, rub it with liquid enzyme detergent, then soak and agitate in cold water for 30 minutes or until the stain is removed.

6. Rinse well.

7. Apply laundry presoak (spot stain remover) and let stand several minutes.

8. Launder according to garment label.

HOUSEHOLD ITEMS *and* MISCELLANY

AMMONIA

GENERAL DESCRIPTION:
A colorless, overwhelmingly pungent gaseous compound, used commercially for refrigeration and the manufacture of chemicals, but for most people mainly encountered as a cleaning agent. Many cleansers sold in supermarkets and drugstores contain ammonia or ammonia compounds. Ammonia gets its name from the salt produced near the oasis of Ammon in Libya.

SEASON:
Spring is perhaps the most common time for this stain, as spring cleaning is a practice that still engages scores of neat freaks across the land. However, since cleaning is not limited to these months, ammonia stains will crop up throughout the year.

AREAS OF OCCURRENCE:
This stain's placement depends on how vigorously you clean. For dedicated scrubbers of floors, the knees of sweatpants or jeans will bear the brunt of this stain. Since cleansers are often liquid or diluted with water and can splash, however, ammonia stains may appear anywhere on T-shirts or sweatshirts as well.

REMOVAL:
1. Rinse the back of the stain thoroughly with cold water.

2. Mix equal amounts of white vinegar and water and sponge the stain with the mixture.

3. Rinse in warm water.

4. Repeat steps 2 through 3 as needed.

5. Launder according to garment label.

BLEACH

GENERAL DESCRIPTION: A chemical agent used to sterilize, whiten, or remove color from a surface or fabric. Bleach stains are one of the most paradoxical, because they're usually acquired when cleaning or when working to remove another stain. A popular brand of bleach in the United States is Clorox, which got its name from combining the words "chlorine" and "sodium hydroxide," two substances that, when mixed, form bleach's active ingredient, sodium hypochlorite.

SEASON:

Since there is always laundry to do, and since there are many stubborn stains that are best treated with bleach, bleach stains may present themselves at any time of year.

AREAS OF OCCURRENCE: Bleach is a dangerous substance that can stain in any number of ways, in any number of areas. If using the bleach as a spot cleaner, you may find that it has removed more than just the color of the offending stain. If you are bleaching an entire load of laundry, chances for accidentally staining socks, colored T-shirts, or a stray pair of pants increase. Because bleach is often sold in large jugs, it tends to splatter when being poured, often staining shirts or pants.

VARIATIONS OF SIGNIFICANCE: Hair bleach; kitchen and bathroom, counter and tile cleaners

REMOVAL: *On fabric:*

 I. Rinse the back of the stain immediately and thoroughly with cold water to neutralize the acid.

2. Place garment on an absorbent cloth and sponge
    well with ammonia, starting from the outside of
    the stain's edge. Replace cloth underneath as it be-
    comes saturated. (If treating stains on wool or silk,
    dilute ammonia with an equal amount of cold wa-
    ter.) If ammonia is not available, substitute a bak-
    ing soda paste, mixing baking soda and water at a
    ratio of approximately 3 to 1. Rub onto stain.

3. Rinse well.

4. Repeat as needed.

5. Launder according to garment label.

On carpet:

1. Sponge the stain immediately with cold water to
    remove as much acid as possible.

2. Mix baking soda and water to make a paste at a ra-
    tio of approximately 3 to 1 and scrub into stain
    with an old toothbrush, then let dry.

3. Repeat steps 1 and 2 until you have removed as
    much stain as possible.

4. Vacuum.

DYES OR RUNNING COLORS

GENERAL
DESCRIPTION: Dye is a coloring material, used on fabric or hair to
                produce a specific hue or tint. Because fabric dye is
                designed to be absorbed into cloth, it becomes a prob-
                lem in the washing machine and dryer. When colors
                run or dyes are transferred from one item of clothing

to another, they can form a stain. Some laundry detergent brands have introduced new products that claim to reduce running colors, or to even absorb extra dye that may "leak" from clothing.

SEASON: Washing clothes, as well as dyeing or tie-dyeing them, is a year-round activity, as is hair coloring; thus, this stain isn't limited to a specific time of year.

AREAS OF OCCURRENCE: When dyeing clothing in your home, you may experience a splash or splatter that affects the clothes you are wearing rather than the item you are dyeing. Therefore a dye stain can appear just about anywhere. When a stain of this nature occurs in the laundry process, it may be everywhere and anywhere, from the backs of blouses to the armpits of a favorite sweater. Hair dye is most likely to appear on the shoulders and necks of shirts, or on pillowcases.

REMOVAL:

1. Dilute bleach according to label and soak the stained garment in a non-metal container for 6 to 8 hours or until the stain is removed. Check first for colorfastness. If color is affected, spread garment over a container in the sink and let cold water slowly drip onto the stain. Drain the container as needed. Continue for 3 to 4 hours.

2. If the stain remains, sponge with equal parts hydrogen peroxide and water and lay garment in the sun. Keep moist with peroxide solution until the stain is gone. Test first for colorfastness.

3. Rinse well, then launder according to garment label.

4. If the stain remains, repeat steps 1 through 3.

FOOD COLORING

GENERAL DESCRIPTION: Natural or synthetic food additives used to alter and intensify color in a processed food. In the U.S. there are only seven artificial colors approved for general use. Food coloring is most often associated with the baking and crafts that accompany any of a number of holidays. Sometimes entire cities can be in on the activity—the city of Chicago started coloring the Chicago River green on St. Patrick's Day in 1962, when 100 pounds of green vegetable dye were added, keeping the water green for a week. Today, 40 pounds of green food coloring keep the river green for a few hours.

SEASON:

Food coloring can be used in crafts year-round, but it is most commonly seen around holidays. Many people color Easter eggs in March and April, staining hands, shirts, carpets, and anything else that might get in the way. Food coloring is also common during the Christmas and Hanukkah baking seasons. A particularly risky day for food-coloring stains is March 17, St. Patrick's Day, when many people add green food coloring to beer to show their true Irish colors (and end up with trails of wayward color on the fronts of their shirts).

AREAS OF OCCURRENCE:

In addition to the potential targets noted above, you should be careful of your apron, tablecloth, carpet, and all areas of exposed clothing while coloring Easter eggs, especially when in the company of small children.

TIME OF OCCURRENCE: Most people's baking or craft making that involves food coloring takes place during the day. However, when green beer is involved, the revelry can last from early morning to the wee hours of the following day, when the luck of the Irish just might run out.

<table>
<tr><td>VARIATIONS OF
SIGNIFICANCE:</td><td>Candy; cookies; frosting</td></tr>
</table>

REMOVAL: *On fabric:*

1. Treat the stain as soon as possible. Hold stain upside down under a stream of cold water to force food coloring out of fabric. Continue until no more coloring is removed.

2. If the stain remains, rub a liquid enzyme detergent into it and let stand several minutes. Agitate the fabric, rubbing the stain between your thumbs.

3. Rinse well in cold water.

4. Repeat steps 2 and 3 until you've removed as much food coloring as possible.

5. Apply laundry presoak (spot stain remover) and let stand several minutes.

6. Launder according to garment label.

7. If the stain remains, mix equal parts of hydrogen peroxide and water and sponge mixture onto stain. Place stain in sunlight and keep moist with peroxide solution until the stain is removed.

8. Rinse well.

On carpet:

1. Blot stain well with an absorbent cloth.

2. Sponge the stain with club soda or cold water. Repeat until you have removed as much stain as possible.

3. Treat with a carpet spotter, according to manufacturer's directions.

⚠ 4. If the stain remains, blot with a mild bleach such as hydrogen peroxide or lemon juice, then sponge with cold water. Repeat as needed.

FURNITURE POLISH

GENERAL DESCRIPTION: A substance that protects and beautifies fine woodwork and antiques, offering smoothness or gloss. Most commercial polishes contain petroleum distillates, which are harmful when inhaled. You can, however, make your own natural furniture polish by combining two parts vegetable or olive oil with one part lemon juice. (See Oil, Cooking or Vegetable on page 86 and Lemon Juice on page 29.) Any polish you use should be rubbed onto finished furniture in the direction of the grain, using a soft, lint-free cloth.

AREAS OF OCCURRENCE: Furniture polish is generally sold in spray cans or bottles. The area of the stain may depend on which type you choose. Spray cans will likely not cause as many stains as the bottled types of polish, but misdirected spray can mar the fronts of T-shirts and pants. Bottled polish is more difficult to control, and will therefore stain more frequently. Sleeves and elbows of sweatshirts and T-shirts are most vulnerable to this stain, especially when polishing is vigorous.

TIME OF OCCURRENCE:	Any time furniture becomes dull, dingy, or scratched is a time when this stain can occur.
REMOVAL:	*On fabric:*

1. Blot excess with absorbent cloth.

2. Spray stain with WD-40™ and let stand for 10 minutes.

3. Sponge with dishwashing liquid and tepid water, occasionally rubbing the stain between your thumbs.

4. Rinse well.

5. Repeat steps 2 through 4 until you have removed as much stain as possible.

6. If the stain remains, apply a laundry presoak (spot stain remover) and let stand several minutes.

7. Launder in the hottest water safe for the fabric.

8. If a color stain remains, dilute bleach according to label and soak the stained garment in a non-metal container for 6 to 8 hours or until the stain is removed. Check first for colorfastness. If color is affected, spread garment over a container in the sink and let cold water slowly drip onto the stain. Drain the container as needed. Continue for 3 to 4 hours.

9. If the stain remains, sponge with equal parts hydrogen peroxide and water and lay garment in the sun. Keep moist with peroxide solution until the stain is gone. Test first for colorfastness.

10. Rinse well and launder according to garment label.

On carpet:

1. Blot excess with an absorbent cloth.

2. Sponge with dishwashing liquid and tepid water.

3. Scrub soapy mixture lightly into stain with an old toothbrush.

4. Blot with a damp cloth.

5. Repeat steps 2 through 4 until you have removed as much as possible.

6. Sponge with clean water, then blot with a dry cloth.

7. If the stain remains, treat with a carpet spotter according to manufacturer's directions.

GUM

GENERAL DESCRIPTION:
A sweetened, flavored substance for chewing, originally made from a tree latex called chicle. Modern chewing gum was created when an American inventor tried (and failed) to develop chicle, which South Americans had been chewing for centuries, into a substitute rubber. The stretchier bubble gum variety is traditionally pink, which is credited to chance—the inventor had only red coloring left, and the color has "stuck" through the years. Gum's sticky nature doesn't affect only fabric—many people encounter the disastrous problem of removing chewing gum from hair. The most reliable method—aside from using scissors—involves peanut butter. Massage a small amount of

peanut butter—preferably smooth, though chunky will work—into the gum until it is loose enough to remove. Then you must battle the peanut butter in your hair. (See Peanut Butter on page 49.)

SEASON:

Chewing gum will adhere to clothes, carpets, and furniture regardless of season, but there is an increased chance of encountering the substance during the school year, when children are likely to try to hide gum from strict teachers and principals. Another time when the incidence of this stain may be higher is in January, when New Year's resolutions are in place and smokers are desperate to kick the habit.

AREAS OF OCCURRENCE:

Gum is most often found on shoes, the seats of pants, and chairs and other upholstered furniture, though strings of gum might stick anywhere. No parts of pants, fronts of shirts, dresses, and school uniforms are safe. Gum can also be found on bedsheets and pillowcases if you fall asleep with gum in your mouth.

TIME OF OCCURRENCE:

School hours, from about 8 a.m. to 3 p.m., are the most common time for gum to stick to clothing and other materials, but any time someone is fighting the urge for a smoke can also create a sticky situation.

VARIATIONS OF SIGNIFICANCE:

Bubble gum ice cream

REMOVAL:

On fabric:

1. Place an ice cube in a plastic bag and rub over the gum until it hardens. (Or place entire garment in the freezer.)

2. Use a dull knife or spoon to remove as much as possible.

3. If the stain remains, treat it with a laundry presoak (spot stain remover) and let stand several minutes.

4. Rub a liquid laundry detergent into the stain and launder according to garment label.

5. If the stain remains, repeat step 3, then launder with a bleach that is safe for the fabric.

On carpet:

1. Place an ice cube in a plastic bag and rub over the gum until it hardens. Use a dull knife or spoon to remove as much as possible.

2. If the stain remains, treat with a carpet spotter. Use according to manufacturer's directions.

HYDROGEN PEROXIDE

GENERAL DESCRIPTION: A viscous, nearly colorless liquid used (in diluted form) for disinfecting and bleaching. There's nothing better for use on a cut or scrape than hydrogen peroxide, even though it stings when applied. Hydrogen peroxide is toxic, but your body creates a small amount of it naturally, both as a byproduct of other processes and to signal your immune system when you are injured and need to fight infection. (Since hydrogen peroxide is poisonous, your body also creates the enzymes that break it down. This is why a piece of liver will foam if you pour diluted peroxide on it.)

SEASON:

Since there is no prescribed time of year for mishaps resulting in skin abrasions, there is no set season when a hydrogen peroxide stain will be more likely. The exception might be summer, when the number of cuts and scrapes may rise with the temperature, since shorts are worn and children play outside more at that time.

AREAS OF OCCURRENCE:

When treating a scrape on the knee with the stuff, the rolled up cuffs of pant legs or the hems of shorts will be most affected by this stain. When hair dye is unavailable, hydrogen peroxide works to bleach hair. In this instance, the stain will be found on the collar area of whatever type of shirt is worn during the dyeing process.

REMOVAL:

On fabric:

1. Rinse the back of the stain thoroughly as soon as possible with cold water to neutralize the acid.

2. Place garment on an absorbent cloth and sponge well with ammonia, starting from the outside of the stain's edge. Replace cloth underneath as it becomes saturated. (If treating stains on wool or silk, dilute ammonia with an equal amount of cold water.) If ammonia is not available, substitute a baking soda paste, mixing baking soda and water at a ratio of approximately 3 to 1. Rub into stain.

3. Rinse well.

4. Repeat as needed.

5. Launder according to garment label.

On carpet:

1. Sponge the stain immediately with cold water to remove as much acid as possible.

2. Mix baking soda and water to make a paste at a ratio of approximately 3 to 1 and scrub into stain with an old toothbrush, then let dry.

3. Repeat steps 1 and 2 until you have removed as much stain as possible.

 4. Vacuum.

IODINE

GENERAL DESCRIPTION
The antiseptic we call "iodine" is actually a solution of iodine in ethyl alcohol; iodine itself is a shiny dark grey element that looks like metal under normal conditions (although it's not technically a metal). Iodine gets its name from the Greek word *ioeides*, meaning "violet," since it turns into a violet-colored vapor when heated. Undiluted iodine can be toxic and irritating to the skin, but iodine solutions are used to clean wounds. The element is also crucial for thyroid functioning, and iodized salt has been a major global public health measure, reducing goiters, hypothyroidism, and deficiency-based developmental disorders.

SEASON:

Summertime is iodine season. You are most likely to encounter scrapes, cuts, and scratches during this active time of year, when working or playing outdoors. Of course, the less graceful among us can encounter such scrapes and cuts regardless of the season, and there are few who can escape a paper cut during the dry winter months. Iodine transcends season in these instances—it is a stain-maker for all seasons.

AREAS OF OCCURRENCE:

Iodine stains aren't just found on the lab coats of chemists. Stains can sneak out from underneath bandages on any part of the body, but most likely on knees, elbows, and other scrape-prone areas, to stain shorts and T-shirts. Bedsheets are at particular risk for iodine stains because, in the quest to let a wound breathe, you may not bandage a wound that has been covered in iodine, leading to the morning surprise of stained bed linens.

REMOVAL:

1. Rinse back of stain well with cold water.

2. Place stain-down on an absorbent cloth and blot with sudsy mixture of liquid laundry detergent and water. Replace the cloth beneath as it becomes saturated. Continue until no more iodine is removed.

3. Rinse well.

4. If the stain remains, blot with a mild bleach, such as vinegar, hydrogen peroxide, or lemon juice.

5. Rinse well.

6. Blot again with detergent mixture from step 2.

7. Rinse well.

8. Launder according to garment label.

9. If the stain remains, set in sunlight to dry, then repeat steps 2 through 7.

MEDICINE

GENERAL DESCRIPTION: Any substance used in treating disease or illness. While medication can be found in many forms, such as pills, powder, syrup, and suppository, the only kind that will stain clothing and other fabrics is the syrup. Cough and cold syrups are sold over the counter in most drugstores and come in a variety of strengths and flavors.

SEASON:

Though a cold or cough can be caught any time of year, fall and winter are most often associated with the cold season.

AREAS OF OCCURRENCE:

Since syrups are viscous and those taking them are likely to be at least partially incapacitated due to illness, stains from them can be far-reaching. Dribbled cough syrup is likely to be found on the fronts of T-shirts, pajama tops, and nightgowns, as well as on robes, socks, sheets, and bed linens, depending on the awareness—or lack thereof—of the person administering the fluid.

REMOVAL: *For iron tonics:*

1. Apply a mild bleach, such as lemon juice, to the stain.

2. Sprinkle with salt to absorb stain. For colored fabrics, test first for colorfastness before completing steps 1 and 2.

3. Let fabric sit in direct sunlight. The sun will help to bleach out the stain. Test first for colorfastness.

4. Repeat steps 1 through 3 until stain is removed. Do not let the stain dry between applications.

5. Rinse well in warm water.

6. Launder according to garment label.

7. If the stain remains, treat with a rust remover according to manufacturer's directions.

For alcohol-based medicines:

1. Rinse back of stain well with cold water or club soda.

2. If the stain remains, rub with liquid dishwashing soap or liquid enzyme detergent. Let stand several minutes. (Do not use bar or natural soap of any kind or the stain will set.)

3. Rinse well with cold water.

4. Launder according to garment label.

5. If the stain remains, rub it with liquid enzyme detergent, then soak and agitate in cold water for 30 minutes or until the stain is removed.

6. Rinse well.

7. Apply laundry presoak (spot stain remover) and let stand several minutes.

8. Launder according to garment label.

For oil-based medicines:

1. Use a dull knife or spoon to remove as much as possible.

2. Blot remaining liquid with an absorbent cloth.

3. Sprinkle salt, baking soda, cornstarch, or talcum powder on stain to absorb excess, let stand 10 to 15 minutes, then brush off.

4. Rub colorless dishwashing liquid into stain. Let stand 1 to 2 minutes.

5. Soak in a sudsy mixture of hot water and dishwashing liquid for up to 30 minutes.

6. Rinse the back of the stain well with hot water.

7. Use a dull knife or spoon again to remove any loosened material from the fabric.

8. If the stain remains, repeat steps 3 through 7 until no more can be removed. Alternatively, make a paste of baking soda and water at a ratio of approximately 3 to 1, spread on stain and let dry, then brush off.

9. Apply laundry presoak (spot stain remover) and let stand several minutes to penetrate fabric.

10. Launder in the hottest water safe for the fabric. For extra-heavy stains, replace half the amount of detergent with baking soda.

MILDEW

GENERAL DESCRIPTION: Any of various fungi that form a whitish substance and usually grow on materials like cloth and paper. Mildew is often used interchangeably with the word "mold." Both are generic terms that describe a variety of microorganisms, including fungi, algae, rusts, yeasts, and bacteria. Mildew requires three elements to survive and thrive: a warm climate, a food source, and moisture, making it a natural enemy to campers, homemakers, and college students everywhere.

SEASON: Mildew is prevalent in the warmer periods of the spring, summer, and fall, when both rain and visits to the swimming pool are more likely. These factors alone don't bring the mildew—they work in combo with neglecting to take wet clothes out of your gym bag. Spring, summer, and fall are also seasons for camping, which, with its accompanying lack of clothes dryers and hangers, can provide a fertile breeding ground for mildew.

AREAS OF OCCURRENCE: Mildew does not discriminate. It can manifest anywhere on clothes, towels, jackets, upholstered car seats, in the car trunk, on basement carpeting (or any carpeting that is located in a warm, damp place), on bathroom tiles, and shower curtains.

REMOVAL: *On fabric:*

1. Take garment outside and shake well. Mildew, like other fungi, reproduces via millions of tiny spores. Do not shake a mildewed garment indoors.

2. Soak the stain in cold water until the stain is loosened.

3. Rub liquid laundry detergent into the stain.

4. Launder in the hottest water that is safe for the fabric, with a bleach that is also safe for the fabric.

5. Dry thoroughly, preferably in the sun.

6. If the stain remains, sponge the fabric with lemon juice, sprinkle with salt, then set in the sun to dry.

7. If the stain remains, rinse well and repeat steps 3 through 6.

On tile:

1. Make sure that the room is well ventilated before treating the mildew. Spray a tile cleaner on the tiles and shower curtain according to manufacturer's directions, or pour white vinegar into a spray bottle and spray the tiles and shower curtain.

2. Scrub with a brush or sponge.

3. Rinse well with water.

4. If the stain remains, mix a 10 percent bleach solution and pour it into a spray bottle. Spray the bleach mixture onto the stain. Let stand several minutes, then rinse well with water.

PAINT, ACRYLIC OR WATER-BASED

GENERAL
DESCRIPTION:
Pigment suspended in a liquid medium, applied to various surfaces for purposes of decoration or protec-

tion. Water-based acrylic paints dissolve in water (rather than oil, as in oil-based paints), which makes them a favorite for parents and teachers when painting with children. You have probably experienced an acrylic paint stain at some point in your life, though if it was in your finger painting days, you likely weren't the one who had to fix it. Many house paints are also latex-based acrylics.

SEASON:

Painting the house is generally a spring and summer activity, so stains incurred during this activity will generally happen in those seasons. Artwork, however, knows no season, and stains that arise during this endeavor can happen at any time of year.

AREAS OF OCCURRENCE:

Most people wear either old clothing or protective smocks when painting, but there is still a chance that a stain will appear unexpectedly, especially in the case of a missing "wet paint" sign. Since large surfaces are often painted, stains may appear on the backs as well as on the fronts of T-shirts, sweatshirts, and jeans.

REMOVAL:

For fresh stains on fabric:

1. Use a dull knife or spoon to remove as much as possible.

2. Blot stain with an absorbent cloth. Keep the stain moist for best results.

3. Sponge the stain with a sudsy detergent mixture and rinse. Rub the stain between your thumbs.

4. Rinse well.

5. Repeat steps 3 and 4 until you have removed as much stain as possible.

6. If the stain remains, blot with nail polish remover on an absorbent cloth.

7. Rinse well.

For dried stains on fabric:

1. Brush off as much paint as possible.

2. Apply soapy water or an acrylic paint and varnish remover.

3. Once the stain has softened, use a dull knife or spoon to remove as much as possible. Test first for colorfastness.

4. Rinse well.

5. See steps 2 through 7 for fresh stains.

On carpet:

1. Use a dull knife or spoon to remove as much as possible.

2. Blot stain with an absorbent cloth. Keep the stain moist for best results. If paint has already dried, brush off as much as possible, then apply soapy water or an acrylic paint and varnish remover. Once the stain has softened, use a dull knife or spoon to remove as much as possible. Test first for colorfastness. For large spills, saturate the stain with water and lay towels and other absorbent cloths

over the area to blot. Walk on the towels to help absorb as much paint as possible.

3. Rinse well.

4. Blot the stain with rubbing alcohol.

5. Rinse well.

6. Repeat steps 2 through 5 until you have removed as much stain as possible.

7. If the stain remains, dampen sponge and apply a laundry presoak (spot stain remover). Let stand several minutes.

8. Rinse well.

PAINT, OIL-BASED

GENERAL DESCRIPTION: Pigment suspended in a slow-drying oil, applied almost exclusively to canvas as a means of making art. Many a cleanup in the studio has led to slippery, oily messes (see Oil, Cooking or Vegetable on page 86) because oil paint is difficult to clean. It also lasts longer; the paintings passed down from the great masters were painted with oil-based paints, which now survive not only in the works themselves but in surprising archaeological layers. X-ray radiography of Pablo Picasso's "La Miséreuse accroupie," for instance, revealed that the artist painted his crouching figure over someone else's landscape scene—and that he had originally painted the woman's hand holding a slice of bread, which in the final version is hidden under her cloak.

AREAS OF OCCURRENCE:	Literally any spot on a painter's body is vulnerable to this stain, from the top of a beret to the bottom of a shoe, and anywhere in between.
TIME OF OCCURRENCE:	Artists are forced to act when the muse strikes, therefore the time of a stain's occurrence is not predictable.
REMOVAL:	*For fresh stains on fabric:*

1. Use a dull knife or spoon to remove as much as possible.

2. Blot stain with an absorbent cloth. Keep the stain moist for best results.

3. Rinse well.

4. Place fabric stain side down on an absorbent cloth and sponge the back of the stain with turpentine. Test first for colorfastness. Replace the cloth underneath as it becomes saturated. Continue until no more paint is removed. Do not rinse the stain.

5. Rub liquid laundry detergent into any remaining stain and soak garment in hot water overnight. Occasionally rub the stain between your thumbs during soaking.

6. Rinse well.

7. Launder according to garment label.

8. If the stain remains, apply a laundry presoak (spot stain remover) and let stand several minutes.

9. Launder according to garment label.

For dried stains on fabric:

1. Brush off as much as possible.

2. Read the paint can label to obtain a recommended paint and varnish remover for thinning the paint, then apply.

3. Once the stain has softened, use a dull knife or spoon to remove as much as possible.

4. Follow steps 2 through 9 for fresh stains, above.

On carpet:

⚠ 1. Use a dull knife or spoon to remove as much as possible, then blot stain with an absorbent cloth. Keep the stain moist for best results. If paint has already dried, brush off as much as possible. Read the paint can label to obtain a recommended paint-and-varnish remover for thinning the paint, then apply. Once the stain has softened, use a dull knife or spoon to remove as much as possible. Test first for colorfastness. Rinse well.

⚠ 2. Blot the stain with turpentine. Test first for colorfastness. Blot repeatedly, alternating turpentine and clean water, until most of the stain is removed.

3. Sponge well with clean water.

4. If the stain remains, sponge with dry-cleaning fluid and blot continuously.

5. Sponge a lukewarm sudsy laundry detergent mixture onto the stain and blot until no more stain can be removed.

6. Sponge well with clean water and let carpet dry thoroughly.

 7. Vacuum.

RUST

GENERAL DESCRIPTION:

A reddish, flaky coating formed when iron and other metals are exposed to water or moist air. Though rust weakens metal objects, making them more pliable, it actually increases the weight of the article. Rust is an inevitable result of metal meeting the outdoor elements. This means that there is the potential for a rust stain from just about anywhere: metal stadium seats, metal pipes, the monkey bars on a playground, random gadgets and tools in the garage or basement, and any exposed metal on an old automobile.

SEASON:

In moderate climates, rust stains develop at all times of the year, as the weather takes its toll on any unprotected metallic surface. In climates where rain is limited there is less rust-stain potential—you are less likely to encounter rust in the desert than in a tropical climate.

AREAS OF OCCURRENCE:

Although rust stains can present themselves in any number of places, they are likely to appear on sweatshirts, sweatpants, jeans, and other clothes you might wear when working with plumbing, under the hood of a car, cleaning out the garage, or visiting a stadium with metal seats.

TIME OF OCCURRENCE:

Rust stains are almost always met with a look of surprise from their victims—most people don't think to check under a metal seat before sliding a coat underneath it, and they may not think about the potential for contracting a rust stain when changing a tire. The surprise of finding a rust stain, then, could happen at any time of day.

REMOVAL:

1. Apply a mild bleach, such as lemon juice, to the stain, then sprinkle with salt to absorb it. For colored fabrics, test first for colorfastness.

2. Let fabric sit in direct sunlight. The sun will help to bleach the stain. Test first for colorfastness.

3. Continue to apply lemon juice and salt until the stain is removed. Do not let the stain dry between applications.

4. Rinse well in warm water.

5. Launder according to garment label.

6. If the stain remains, treat with a rust remover according to manufacturer's directions.

SCORCH MARKS

GENERAL DESCRIPTION: Marks caused by slight burning; usually gray or black in color. Scorch marks are extremely common from cooking, camping, ironing, or smoking, and are a particularly pesky stain to remove, since burning fabric can change its chemical makeup.

SEASON:

Since cooking is a year-round activity, scorch marks resulting from this activity will not be limited to any time of year; the same is true of stains resulting from smoking or ironing. Camping, however, is generally a spring and summer activity, and so stains that happen 'round the campfire are limited to those months.

AREAS OF OCCURRENCE: The most common spot for this stain on clothing is the sleeves of a turtleneck, sweatshirt, sweater, or coat. However, the errant ash could find its way onto the fronts of these garments as well, and is even a possibility on trouser legs.

TIME OF OCCURRENCE: A high-risk period is when you smoke or tend a blaze late at night; scorch marks are more prevalent during darkness and in the presence of alcoholic beverages.

REMOVAL: *On light fabric:*

1. Brush off or shake scorched area gently to remove charring.

2. Dampen a piece of white cotton with diluted hydrogen peroxide (at a ratio of 1 part hydrogen peroxide, 4 parts water) and sponge the scorch mark.

3. Let garment dry in the sun for added bleaching.

4. Repeat sponging and drying until no more stain can be removed.

5. Sponge one last time with the peroxide mixture.

6. Cover the mark with a clean, dry, absorbent cloth.

7. Press a medium-warm iron over the cloth. Replace the cloth as the peroxide soaks through. Do not let the iron come into contact with the fabric, since the peroxide can cause rust to form. (If this happens, see Rust on page 146.)

8. If scorch mark remains, repeat steps 2 through 7 until you've removed as much of the scorch mark as possible.

9. Rinse in warm water.

10. Apply a laundry presoak (spot stain remover) and let stand several minutes.

11. Launder according to garment label.

12. If the stain remains, launder with an all-fabric bleach. Test first for colorfastness.

On wool:

1. Sponge the stain with diluted hydrogen peroxide as in step 2 above.

2. Wash in warm water with a little borax powder.

3. Rinse well and air dry.

4. If the stain remains, brush it with an emery board.

SHOE POLISH

GENERAL DESCRIPTION: A substance used to give smoothness or gloss to an external covering for the foot. Shoe polish is a necessity for any style-conscious person, but its uses don't end with the feet. You can also use it to shine, color, and protect wooden furniture, and you can even start a fire with it if you're camping and improbably only have shoe polish. Popular colors include black, brown, blue, and white.

SEASON: Shoe polish stains are year-round occurrences, but the colors vary with the time of year. White shoe polish stains are only incurred in the summer, as long as style guidelines are followed to the letter. Brown and black shoe polish stains should mainly occur in the colder months.

AREAS OF
OCCURRENCE: Pant and shirt cuffs are the areas most affected by this stain. Suit jackets can be marred when the polisher is hurried. In rare instances, pantyhose, socks, and tights may also fall victim to this stain.

TIME OF
OCCURRENCE: Shoes are likely to be polished along with other household chores, so weekends are a likely time for this stain.

REMOVAL:
1. Use a dull knife or spoon to remove as much as possible.

2. Rinse back of stain with cold water, then rub with a bar soap, dishwashing liquid, or liquid laundry detergent. Rub the stain between thumbs.

3. Rinse well.

4. Repeat steps 2 and 3 until no more stain can be removed.

5. If the stain remains, rub with detergent, then soak garment in water for 10 to 15 minutes.

6. Rinse well.

7. If the stain remains, treat with a laundry presoak (spot stain remover) and let stand several minutes.

8. Launder according to garment label.

SOOT OR SMOKE

GENERAL DESCRIPTION:

SOOT: **A black, powdery substance made of incompletely combusted materials.** SMOKE: **A white, gray, or black vapor made from small particles of carbon suspended in air, also produced by combustion.** A perfectly clean fire gives off almost no smoke. Smoke means that a fire is not burning efficiently and that bits of unburned material are escaping. Unfortunately, this perfect fire is uncommon, and smoke, soot, and ash—and their various stains—are present in most (if not all) the fires we encounter. Producing smoke and soot is also a part of the daily rituals of more than one billion smokers worldwide.

SEASON:

Because cigarette smoking is an addiction, it isn't limited to season—stains from cigarettes can be gotten at any time of year, in smokers' homes or cars (road trips can be especially grueling), at all-night diners, and especially near seedy bars. Soot and ash stains are likely in the fall and winter, when you are most likely to clean a fireplace, but the same stains are just as likely in summer from campfires and pit barbecues.

AREAS OF OCCURRENCE:

Soot and ash fly through the air, landing on furniture, carpets, and all imaginable articles of clothing. Purses and bags are not immune to these stains, either. Obviously, the uniforms of firefighters are exposed to these stains—from the top of the hat to the bottom of the boot.

TIME OF OCCURRENCE:

Smoke, soot, and ash are not limited by time of day—heavy smokers indulge their addiction regardless of the hour. If you are a nonsmoker, nighttime activities such as drinking alcohol or lighting campfires increase the chance for acquiring a stain.

REMOVAL: *If the fabric is washable:*

1. Take the fabric outside and gently shake or brush off as much soot as possible. If possible, hold the garment taut and vacuum the stain.

2. Sprinkle an absorbent powder, such as talcum powder, baking soda, or salt, on the stain and let stand for several minutes.

3. Brush off outdoors or vacuum.

4. Repeat steps 2 and 3 until you have removed as much as possible.

5. Apply laundry presoak (spot stain remover) and let stand several minutes.

6. Launder in the hottest water safe for the fabric. For extra-heavy stains, replace half the amount of detergent with baking soda.

If the fabric is not washable:

1. Take the fabric outside and gently shake or brush off as much soot as possible. If possible, hold the garment taut and vacuum the stain.

2. Sponge the stain with dry-cleaning fluid according to manufacturer's directions.

3. Air out as much residual odor as possible by hanging the garment outside or at least out of the closet for a few days.

On carpet:

 1. Vacuum loose particles.

 2. Sprinkle stain with salt and let stand 1 to 2 hours.

 3. Vacuum.

4. Repeat steps 2 and 3 until you have removed as much stain as possible.

5. Apply a carpet spotter according to manufacturer's directions.

TARNISH

GENERAL DESCRIPTION:
A film of oxidation that dulls or discolors a metallic surface. Tarnish can leave an ugly black stain on clothing, and can ruin pots and pans in your kitchen, not to mention silverware and silver pieces in your home. A simple home remedy for cleaning the tarnished bottoms of pots and pans is to spread a little ketchup on the affected surface, and let it sit for about one minute. Wipe clean and rinse, and they're good as new!

SEASON:

Since pots, lamps, and other metallic items tarnish with age, there isn't a particular season when more of this staining happens.

AREAS OF OCCURRENCE:

The sleeves of any clothing worn when cleaning or cooking are vulnerable to this stain, as well as the fronts of these garments. The legs and seat of an old pair of jeans might well be affected, since tarnish transfers easily to hands, which are often wiped carelessly on clothing. This is especially common when polishing silver jewelry or flatware.

<table>
<tr><td>TIME OF OCCURRENCE:</td><td>Because cleaning is an anytime activity, stains encountered when polishing a lamp will not be limited to a specific time of day. Tarnish stains are also frequently incurred during the course of cooking a meal.</td></tr>
</table>

REMOVAL:

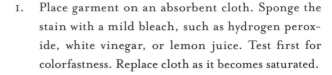

1. Place garment on an absorbent cloth. Sponge the stain with a mild bleach, such as hydrogen peroxide, white vinegar, or lemon juice. Test first for colorfastness. Replace cloth as it becomes saturated.

2. Rinse thoroughly.

3. Repeat steps 1 and 2 until you have removed as much stain as possible.

4. Launder according to garment label.

TOBACCO

GENERAL DESCRIPTION: Tobacco—the prepared leaves of a plant of the genus *Nicotiana*, which are smoked or (less often) chewed or snorted—is probably the oldest addictive drug in existence. It comes in many forms and flavors for smoking and chewing pleasure. Smoking itself has a lore all its own—for example the superstition that it's bad luck to light three cigarettes on the same match. This comes from the British Army, possibly dating to the Boer War (1899–1902); soldiers believed that the flame would give an enemy sniper time to sight his rifle, and the soldier with the third cigarette would invariably be shot.

SEASON: ☼	Serious smokers light up daily, so these stains aren't confined to particular months, though dry tobacco is less likely to stain than chewing tobacco. Chewing tobacco may more frequently stain during the summer baseball season, since a mouthful of chew is a staple of America's pastime. Tobacco from cigars may more often stain during celebrations, such as for the birth of a baby, but these, too, occur throughout the year.
AREAS OF OCCURRENCE:	When rolling your own cigarettes, tobacco is likely to stain the lap areas of jeans and slacks, as well as the fronts of jackets and sweaters. Chewing tobacco is a more far-reaching stain because it involves spitting, so don't be surprised if this brown stain mars shoes, socks, pant legs, and even carpets should you choose to chew.
TIME OF OCCURRENCE:	Tobacco stains are most likely to occur after dark, outside dimly lit bars or restaurants, though they won't be limited to this time; most smokers enjoy their tobacco throughout the day.
VARIATIONS OF SIGNIFICANCE:	Chewing tobacco; cigarettes; cigars
REMOVAL:	1. Brush off excess material outdoors.
	2. Use a dull knife or spoon to remove as much as possible.
	3. Rinse the back of the stain well with cold water.
	4. Blot with an absorbent cloth.
	5. Treat with a laundry presoak (spot stain remover) and let stand 20 to 30 minutes. For tough stains,

first rub with glycerin and let stand until the stain is softened, then apply a laundry presoak.

 6.   Launder according to garment label.

WATER SPOTS

GENERAL DESCRIPTION:
Spots left by water on delicate fabrics such as silk, fine wool, or rayon. It may take 100 drops of water to fill a teaspoon, but it only takes one errant drop to damage a fine silk blouse. Water is usually the substance you use to remove stains, thus it seems paradoxical to concern ourselves with removing stains incurred by this very agent—but water contains minerals, which can be left behind when fabric is splashed and dries slowly.

SEASON:
The period of highest risk for developing water spots is during the seasons when weather is most active—in moderate climates, usually winter and spring. There is some chance of finding these spots year round, especially for those who are very concerned about their outward appearance and use steam irons to smooth wrinkles in their clothes.

AREAS OF OCCURRENCE:

Water spots can present themselves anywhere on a garment if acquired through ironing. If acquired during a rain or snow storm, the fronts and backs of shirts, pants, dresses, sweaters, coats, and jackets are most at risk, and the arms and shoulders of these garments will almost certainly need to be treated.

REMOVAL: *On silk, rayon, or wool:*

  1.   Fill a kettle with water and bring to a boil. Cover the spout with cheesecloth to prevent water droplets from splattering out.

2.   Once the water is boiling, hold the stained fabric over the steam until it becomes damp, but not wet.

3.   Shake and press the fabric while it is still damp. Rub the affected area with a spoon or other dull surface.

On carpet:

1.   Blot as much of the spill as possible. Lay absorbent cloths over the stain and walk on them to absorb excess liquid.

2.   Dry the stain as quickly as possible by covering the spill with sheets of absorbent material, such as paper towels or blotting paper. Stack books on top of the absorbent sheets. Point a fan at the spill. (Never use a radiator as the heat can cause some carpet to scorch and shrink.) As the water dries, it will be forced up into the sheets. Replace the sheets as they become saturated.

or

If possible, prop the carpet up and aim a fan at the stain to dry both sides (top and bottom). If you can take the carpet up, it is recommended that you have a professional reinstall and steam-clean it.

WAX, CANDLE

GENERAL DESCRIPTION: A solid substance made of fats or oils (including fatty acids secreted by honeybees), which has been molded, embedded with a wick, often scented and dyed, and lit by humans to provide light and/or aroma. Though candles functioned at one time as a strictly utilitarian device, they have now become synonymous with romance and good decorating.

SEASON:
❄

Candles are burned throughout the year for their warm glow and pleasing scents at romantic dinners and parties alike. There is perhaps an increase in candle stains during Hanukkah, when the menorah burns for eight days, and at birthday parties, especially when the guest of honor is of advanced years, requiring more candles.

AREAS OF OCCURRENCE:

Dripping wax can be quite far-reaching, especially when the candle itself is being blown out. Too forceful an exhalation and the hot wax will splatter everywhere; it can stain evening gowns, tuxedos, sweaters, and jeans as well as wallpaper, carpets, tables, and curtains.

TIME OF OCCURRENCE: The most common time for a wax stain to develop is after dark, when romance is in the air.

VARIATIONS OF SIGNIFICANCE: Birthday cakes; lanterns; menorahs

REMOVAL: *On fabric:*

I. Put an ice cube in a plastic bag and rub the wax until it is brittle, or place the entire garment in the freezer. Peel off as much wax as possible.

2. If a residue remains, lay an absorbent cloth or un-printed side of a brown paper bag over the stain.

3. Gently press the cloth with a warm iron. The wax will melt and seep into cloth. If cloth begins to brown, replace with a fresh cloth. Continue to iron until the wax has been completely absorbed by the cloth.

4. If the candle is colored and the wax has left a dye stain, blot it with rubbing alcohol.

5. If the stain remains, apply a laundry presoak (spot stain remover) and let stand several minutes.

6. Launder according to garment label.

On hard surfaces, such as wood, tiles, or paneling:

1. Put an ice cube in a plastic bag and rub the wax until it is brittle. Peel off as much wax as possible.

2. If a residue remains, lay an absorbent cloth or un-printed side of a brown paper bag over the stain.

3. Gently press the cloth with a warm iron. The wax will melt and seep into cloth. If the cloth begins to brown, replace with a fresh cloth. Continue to iron until the wax has been completely absorbed by the cloth.

4. If a dye stain remains, wipe with rubbing alcohol. Rinse surface with water.

YELLOWING

GENERAL DESCRIPTION: The process by which fabrics turn yellow after a period of time. Some yellowed clothing may inspire a wave of nostalgia—a christening gown, a wedding dress, a prom dress, a military uniform, or a graduation gown are just a few examples. After the wedding, many brides opt to seal their gowns to protect the garments from signs of aging and other damaging threats. However, sealing a gown in a plastic bag can actually accelerate the aging process, because fumes from the plastic contribute to yellowing.

SEASON: Yellowing occurs over a period of time, so there is no season during which you can be more vigilant to prevent it. You are most likely to discover the yellowing during spring cleaning, around anniversaries when nostalgia requires a peek into the past, and in the dead of winter, when cabin fever causes many to resort to cleaning out closets for entertainment.

AREAS OF OCCURRENCE: Yellowing can affect an entire garment, though it is most likely to occur under the arms of shirts, jackets, and dresses because of a combination of substances in your sweat and substances in your antiperspirant. Because only white clothing yellows noticeably, yellowing is most likely to affect items such as bed linens, work shirts, and special-occasion garments such as wedding gowns.

REMOVAL:
I. Fill a bucket with warm water. Add denture-cleaning tablets according to manufacturer's directions.

2. Once the tablets are dissolved, add stained garment and soak until the yellowing is gone.

3. Rinse well.

4. Launder according to garment label.

GARAGE
and YARD

CHARCOAL

GENERAL DESCRIPTION: A form of carbon produced when an organic substance like wood is burned or heated in an environment with limited air. A necessity at any barbecue that doesn't involve a gas or electric grill, charcoal briquettes were invented (or at least monetized) by Henry Ford. While barbecues are the most obvious and common use for charcoal, it can also be used to create artistic master-pieces—which may be its most stain-inducing applica-tion, especially if you're left-handed.

SEASON: Summer is prime time for charcoal stains, since it's the best time for barbecues on the hibachi. Charcoal is used in artwork year-round, so stains from this are not confined to any particular time of year.

AREAS OF OCCURRENCE: Since charcoal smudges easily, its stains can be far-reaching. The front of your apron or smock is a prime target, as are the sleeves of your T-shirt or sweater. Since hands are vulnerable to charcoal accu-mulation, and the legs and seats of jeans and trousers are the easiest places to wipe hands clean, these areas of clothing often show charcoal stains.

REMOVAL:
1. Take the fabric outside and gently shake or brush off as much charcoal as possible. If possible, hold the garment taut and vacuum the stain.

2. Sprinkle an absorbent powder, such as talcum powder, baking soda, or salt, on the stain and let stand for several minutes.

3. Brush off outdoors or vacuum.

4. Repeat steps 2 and 3 until you have removed as much stain as possible.

5. Rinse the back of the stain with warm water.

6. Apply laundry presoak (spot stain remover) and let stand several minutes.

7. Launder in the hottest water safe for the fabric. For extra-heavy stains, replace half the amount of detergent with baking soda.

DIRT OR MUD

GENERAL DESCRIPTION:

DIRT: **Earth or soil, the mixture of disintegrated rock and organic matter in which plants grow.** MUD: **Soft earth that has been saturated with water.** An unusual eating disorder called pica, blamed on iron deficiency anemia, may cause sufferers to have an overwhelming desire to eat dirt (or tomatoes, ice, detergent, starch, clay, or even rocks). Those who give in to these cravings open themselves up not only to sickness but to some nasty stain possibilities.

SEASON:

Every season has its own type of dirt or mud, for example: winter slush, spring gardening dirt, summer silt from swimming in lakes or creeks, and fall mud from a wet football field. No time of year is safe.

AREA OF OCCURRENCE:

Stains from dirt and mud can coat any area of the body, especially shoes, socks, and the cuffs of pants. Mud from a roadside can splash all over your best dress, slacks, or jacket; a muddy sports field can coat a uniform with half the field by the end of a game. And carpets are perhaps the most vulnerable of all possible surfaces to a dirt or mud stain.

TIME OF OCCURRENCE: There is no time of day or night when dirt and mud are not stain hazards.

VARIATIONS OF SIGNIFICANCE: Houseplant soil

REMOVAL: *If the fabric is washable:*

1. Let stain dry completely. Do not smear or wipe it while wet; this will only set and spread the stain.

2. Once dry, shake the stain to remove as much dirt as possible. Or vacuum the fabric.

3. Rub liquid enzyme detergent into the stain, then soak in water for 10 to 20 minutes or until the stain is gone. Rub the stain between thumbs occasionally during soaking. Older stains may need to be soaked for several hours.

4. If the stain remains, apply a laundry presoak (spot stain remover) and let stand several minutes.

5. Launder with enzyme detergent.

6. If the stain remains, repeat step 3.

7. Blot remaining color stain with white vinegar or hydrogen peroxide.

8. Rinse well.

9. Launder according to garment label.

If the fabric is not washable:

1. Let stain dry completely. Do not smear or wipe it while wet.

2. Once dry, shake the stain to remove as much dirt as possible. Or vacuum the fabric.

3. Mix a sudsy solution of liquid enzyme detergent and water, and sponge mixture onto stain.

4. Rinse stained area with water.

5. Repeat as needed.

On carpet:

1. Sprinkle stain with salt, baking soda, or other absorbent powder and let dry.

2. Vacuum.

3. Repeat until you have removed as much stain as possible.

4. Treat with a carpet spotter according to manufacturer's directions.

GASOLINE

GENERAL DESCRIPTION: A flammable liquid derived from petroleum, primarily used as fuel for internal combustion engines. With its unmistakable smell and myriad uses, gasoline is easily the most popular fuel around—your car or boat couldn't live without it. Gasoline does not burn; rather, it emits gasses that burn. Due to cleaner burning gasoline (especially the removal of lead) and improved technology, today's new cars produce roughly 99 percent less common pollution than a model from 1970.

SEASON:

Filling up the tank of your SUV or sports car is a year-round activity, but you'll usually fill your speedboat with gas in the summertime, making this stain slightly more probable during the warmer months.

AREAS OF OCCURRENCE:

It is illegal to pump your own gas in the states of New Jersey and Oregon; therefore, the motorists in those states are virtually immune to this stinky stain. Running out of gas on the side of the road can happen anywhere, however, and cans of gasoline are unwieldy. When using a gas can, as when using a gas pump, you are bound to occasionally splash the liquid onto shoes, socks, or the cuffs of trousers.

TIME OF OCCURRENCE:

A gas station attendant or motorist may encounter this stain any time of day or night, as thoughtful proprietors know that fuel is always needed, and many stations are open 24 hours a day.

REMOVAL:

On fabric:

1. Use a dull knife or spoon to remove as much as possible.

2. Blot remaining liquid with an absorbent cloth.

3. Sprinkle salt, baking soda, cornstarch, or talcum powder on stain to absorb excess liquid, let stand 10 to 15 minutes, then brush off.

4. Rub colorless dishwashing liquid into the stain. Let stand 1 to 2 minutes.

5. Soak in a sudsy mixture of hot water and dish-washing liquid for up to 30 minutes.

6. Rinse the back of the stain well with hot water.

7. Use a dull knife or spoon to remove any loosened grease or oil from the fabric.

8. If the stain remains, repeat steps 3 through 7.

9. If the stain remains, make a paste of baking soda and water at a ratio of approximately 3 to 1, spread on the stain and let dry, then brush off.

10. Apply laundry presoak (spot stain remover) and let stand several minutes.

11. Launder in the hottest water safe for the fabric. For extra-heavy stains, replace half the amount of detergent with baking soda.

12. If the stain remains, repeat steps 2 through 7.

On carpet:

1. Use a dull knife or spoon to remove as much as possible.

2. Blot remaining liquid with an absorbent cloth. (For heavy or dark stains, it is best to call a professional cleaner.)

3. Sprinkle the stain with an absorbent powder, such as baking soda, cornstarch, cornmeal, or talcum powder. Let sit for 6 to 12 hours, then vacuum (do not brush) the powder.

or

Spray with shaving cream and work it into the carpet with an old toothbrush. Wipe with a damp cloth, then sponge with cold water.

or

Dampen with club soda and blot gently. Repeat as needed.

4. If the stain remains, apply dry-cleaning fluid (be careful not to wet the carpet backing with it), then sponge the stain with a damp cloth.

or

Treat with a carpet spotter according to manufacturer's directions.

GRASS

GENERAL DESCRIPTION:

Any of the narrow-leafed plants from the family *Gramineae* that are used as ground cover in residential and public recreational spaces, as well as most undeveloped land in temperate climates. Nearly unavoidable during times of moderate weather, this plant is frequently the object of obsession for suburban homeowners (and homeowners' associations). Grass grows quickly when watered; hence, many people regularly trim it to a comfortable height of, on average, about three inches.

SEASON:

Grass stains appear during periods of moderate weather when you are likely to be spending time outdoors. Grass stains rarely appear in winter, except during an occasional particularly bad spill from a sled, or in areas where the climate is moderate year-round.

AREAS OF
OCCURRENCE:

The most obvious spots for grass stains are the seats and knees of pants, the seats of skirts and shorts, and the elbows of jackets and long-sleeved shirts, depending on how comfortable the wearers become in the grass. Baseball, softball, and soccer players acquire grass stains on all areas of their uniforms, especially when sliding to base or defending the goal. When mowing the grass be particularly conscious of the cuffs of pant legs.

TIME OF
OCCURRENCE:

Most outdoor activities, and thus most grass stains, occur when the sun is shining. Stains acquired while mowing the lawn probably occur most often in the early morning when your neighbors are trying to sleep, a favorite time of day for this activity.

VARIATIONS OF
SIGNIFICANCE:

Floral arrangements; golf greens; mulch from grass clippings

REMOVAL:

1. Place garment stain side down on absorbent cloth and sponge back of stain with rubbing alcohol, replacing pad underneath as needed. Test first for colorfastness. (For acetate fabrics, dilute alcohol with 2 parts water. Do not use alcohol on wool.)

2. Rinse well in cold water.

3. If the stain remains, use an old toothbrush to scrub the stain with non-gel toothpaste (preferably containing baking soda). Let stand for 2 to 3 minutes. If toothpaste is not available, sponge the stain with white vinegar.

4. Rinse well.

5. If the stain remains, repeat steps 1 through 4 until you've removed as much stain as possible.

6. Rub the stain with laundry presoak (spot stain remover) and let stand for several minutes.

7. Launder with a liquid enzyme detergent.

Very heavy, stubborn, remaining stains can also be treated as a Dyes or Running Colors stain. See page 124.

GREASE

GENERAL DESCRIPTION:
Fatty or oily matter in general; lubricant. In 1400 B.C. affluent Egyptian women wore cones of scented grease on top of their heads. As the day wore on, the hot sun would melt the grease, causing it to drip down their bodies, covering their skin with a glistening sheen, and saturating their clothes with fragrance. In contemporary times, grease is more likely to be used as a lubricant in cars and other mechanical devices than as a vehicle for perfume.

SEASON:
Grease stains can present themselves at any time, especially if you are mechanically inclined or work around lots of moving parts.

AREAS OF OCCURRENCE:
People who work around cars and other machines that employ grease as a lubricant often have special clothes, like jumpsuits or coveralls, to protect other pieces of clothing from damaging stains. These protective garments are of course vulnerable to staining in any loca-

tion. People who do not work around grease are not immune, however—the edges of car doors are notorious for preying on the clothing of an unsuspecting victim, especially in the arm or buttocks region. Bicycle riders should also beware, as grease from the chain can easily stain socks and pants cuffs.

VARIATIONS OF SIGNIFICANCE: Bicycle chains; car doors; greased hinges

REMOVAL: *On fabric:*

1. Use a dull knife or spoon to remove as much as possible.

2. Blot remaining liquid with an absorbent cloth.

3. Sprinkle salt, baking soda, cornstarch, or talcum powder on stain to absorb excess grease and let stand 15 to 30 minutes, then brush off. Repeat until you have removed as much stain as possible.

4. Rub colorless dishwashing liquid into stain. Let stand 1 to 2 minutes.

5. Soak in hot water for up to 30 minutes.

6. Rinse the back of the stain well with hot water.

7. Use a dull knife or spoon again to remove any loosened grease from the fabric.

8. Blot with an absorbent cloth.

9. If the stain remains, make a paste of baking soda and water at a ratio of approximately 3 to 1, spread on stain and let dry, then brush off.

10. Apply laundry presoak (spot stain remover) and let stand several minutes.

11. Launder in the hottest water safe for the fabric. For extra-heavy stains, replace half the amount of detergent with baking soda.

12. If the stain remains, repeat steps 3 through 11.

On carpet:

1. Use a dull knife or spoon to remove as much as possible.

2. Blot remaining liquid with an absorbent cloth. (For heavy or dark stains, it is best to call a professional cleaner.)

3. Sprinkle the stain with an absorbent powder, such as baking soda, cornstarch, cornmeal, or talcum powder. Let sit for 6 to 12 hours, then vacuum (do not brush) the powder.

or

Spray with shaving cream and work it into the carpet with an old toothbrush. Wipe it off with a damp cloth, then sponge with cold water.

or

Dampen with club soda and blot gently. Repeat as needed.

4. If the stain remains, apply dry-cleaning fluid (be careful not to wet the carpet backing with it), then sponge the stain with a damp cloth.

or

Treat with a carpet spotter according to manufacturer's directions.

On wallpaper or walls:

1. Make a paste of cornstarch or baking soda and water at a ratio of approximately 3 to 1, then smear
   the paste onto stain. Non-gel toothpaste can also
   be used. Let paste dry, then wipe with a clean
   cloth. For toothpaste, let stand 10 to 15 minutes,
   then wipe with a damp cloth.

2. Repeat until the stain is gone.

OIL, MOTOR

GENERAL
DESCRIPTION:
A thick, viscous, combustible liquid of refined petroleum, used in the maintenance of automobiles and
other moving machinery. Bottled motor oil, which is
available at most filling stations and garages, allows
more and more people to add and change their own
oil, so this stain is not limited to mechanics and gas
station attendants. However, car enthusiasts and professionals alike should take care with this dark, sticky
substance, as it is extremely toxic. A mere quart of
motor oil can pollute 250,000 gallons of water.

SEASON:

Because oil changes are supposed to be done every several thousand miles or every few months (whichever
comes first), stains from the process are not more
prevalent in a particular season.

AREAS OF OCCURRENCE:

Depending on how they are obtained, motor oil stains can appear anywhere on your person. After a long day at the garage, mechanics may look as though they have bathed in the stuff, finding it all over the sleeves, legs, fronts, and backs of their jumpsuits, not to mention on skin, hair, and in ears. The backs of shirts, sweaters, pants, and jackets are particularly susceptible when you are lying down in a driveway, under a car. If you trip in a parking lot on a hot day, motor oil stains are likely to show up on the knees and/or seat of your jeans or slacks.

TIME OF OCCURRENCE:

A garage attendant, mechanic, or motorist can obtain this stain any time of day or night, as oil changes or additions are not limited to daytime, and many stations are open 24 hours. After a particularly messy day, a mechanic or automobile enthusiast may even transfer these nasty stains to carpets or walls upon returning home.

REMOVAL:

On fabric:

1. Use a dull knife or spoon to remove as much as possible.

2. Blot remaining liquid with an absorbent cloth.

3. Sprinkle salt, baking soda, cornstarch, or talcum powder on stain to absorb excess oil, let stand 10 to 15 minutes, then brush off.

4. Rub colorless dishwashing liquid into stain. Let stand 1 to 2 minutes.

5. Soak in a sudsy mixture of hot water and dishwashing liquid for up to 30 minutes.

6. Rinse the back of the stain well with hot water.

7. Use a dull knife or spoon to remove any loosened oil from the fabric.

8. If the stain remains, make a paste of baking soda and water at a ratio of approximately 3 to 1, spread on stain and let dry, then brush off.

9. Apply laundry presoak (spot stain remover) and let stand several minutes to penetrate fabric.

10. Launder in the hottest water safe for the fabric. For extra-heavy stains, replace half the amount of detergent with baking soda.

11. If the stain remains, repeat steps 3 through 10.

On carpet:

1. Use a dull knife or spoon to remove as much as possible.

2. Blot remaining liquid with an absorbent cloth. (For heavy or dark stains, it is best to call a professional cleaner.)

3. Sprinkle the stain with an absorbent powder such as baking soda, cornstarch, cornmeal, or talcum powder. Let sit for 6 to 12 hours, then vacuum (do not brush) the powder.

or

Spray with shaving cream and work it into the carpet with an old toothbrush. Wipe it off with a damp cloth, then sponge with cold water.

or

> Dampen with club soda and blot gently. Repeat as needed.

4. If the stain remains, apply dry-cleaning fluid (be careful not to wet the carpet backing with it), then sponge the stain with a damp cloth.

or

> Treat with a carpet spotter according to manufacturer's directions.

On wallpaper or walls:

1. Make a paste of baking soda and water at a ratio of approximately 3 to 1, then smear the paste onto stain. Non-gel toothpaste can also be used. Let paste dry, then wipe off. For toothpaste, let stand 10 to 15 minutes, then wipe off with a damp cloth.

2. Repeat until the stain is gone.

POLLEN

GENERAL DESCRIPTION: A powdery substance, often yellow, found in flowering plants; part of the plant reproductive cycle. Some plants, especially orchids, use sneaky mimicry to spread their pollen, luring insects to their flowers with structures or scents that suggest food or a mate. When the insect lands, hoping for either a snack bounty or a roll in the hay, they get covered in the flower's pollen, which they then transmit to other plants, because bugs don't learn quickly.

Hay fever sufferers know that pollen is in season during spring and summer in most climates. You may acquire pollen stains when working in the garden or tending to fresh flowers. Pay attention to those beautiful lilies in early spring, with their huge stamens quivering with pollen, ready to inflict a bright yellow spot on your finest spring attire. Pollen has become popular as a source of natural vitamins and minerals, increasing the chances for year-round staining.

AREAS OF
OCCURRENCE:

Pollen can stain pant legs and skirts as you wander through the garden or across a field of goldenrod. Pollen can also color shirt sleeves and fronts, particularly when you are flower arranging. In early summer, trees drop pollen all over streets and cars, making this stain nearly impossible to avoid, as it shows up on shoes, socks, and even jackets and pants.

REMOVAL:

1. Shake garment outdoors to remove loose pollen.

2. Use a dull knife or spoon to remove as much as possible.

3. Rinse the back of the stain well with cold water.

4. Soak garment in cold water until the stain is loosened.

5. Rinse well.

6. Repeat steps 3 through 5 until you have removed as much stain as possible.

7. If the stain remains, apply a laundry presoak (spot stain remover) and let stand several minutes.

8. Launder in the hottest water safe for the fabric.

SAP

GENERAL DESCRIPTION: The watery fluid that circulates through a plant's vascular tissues, distributing water, minerals, and nutrients. Sugar-maple tree sap is the basic ingredient for the popular maple syrup, but maples are not the only trees that can produce edible sap products. Palm tree sap can be used to make palm syrup, and birch sap (including fermented, alcoholic birch sap) is a traditional drink in a number of Eastern European countries.

SEASON:

Because the sap used to make maple syrup is generally collected in early spring, an increase in sap stains at that time of year is to be expected. However, since plants and trees release sap year-round, tree huggers, tree surgeons, and loggers, as well as gardeners and nursery workers, must be vigilant throughout the year.

AREAS OF OCCURRENCE:

If you operate on or climb a tree, the legs of your jeans and trousers most certainly are vulnerable to this stain. The cuffs, sleeves, and fronts of jackets and sweaters are also prime targets. Plant sap also finds its way onto gardening gloves, smocks, and sweatshirts. While sap is being collected for maple syrup, shoes, socks, boots, and the legs of pants are all common stain areas.

TIME OF OCCURRENCE: Most stains from this sticky liquid are experienced during daylight hours, when tree surgeries and sap-collecting most often take place.

REMOVAL:

1. Use a dull knife or spoon to remove as much as possible.

2. Rub glycerin into the stain and let stand several minutes until sap is softened. For old stains, warm the glycerin, spread it over the stain, and let stand.

3. Place stain over an absorbent cloth and tap the back of it with an old toothbrush to loosen the stain. Replace the cloth as it becomes saturated. Continue until you have removed as much as possible.

4. If a color stain remains, apply a laundry presoak (spot stain remover) and let stand several minutes.

5. Launder according to garment label.

TAR OR ASPHALT

GENERAL DESCRIPTION:

TAR: **A dark viscous liquid made of carbon and hydrocarbons, produced from coal, wood, peat, or other organic material.** ASPHALT: **Also known as bitumen; a dark, sticky, viscous liquid or semisolid petroleum, which is mixed with gravel or other particles for paving.** Tar is primarily used to weatherproof and seal things like boat hulls and roof shingles, while asphalt is used for roads; it's preferred to concrete because it is less expensive and more flexible. When water freezing underground causes the earth to expand, an asphalt-paved road will expand with it, while a concrete-paved road will crack.

| SEASON: | For the general public, tar and asphalt stains occur almost exclusively during the warm months of late spring, summer, and early fall. These substances are solid when they're cold, so there is little risk of them spreading and smearing during the winter months. However, construction workers may be susceptible to the stains year-round, when roofing, filling potholes, or paving new roads. |

| AREA OF OCCURRENCE: | Tar and asphalt stick readily to shoes, socks, and cuffs of pants. Stains on knees and elbows are also possible, especially following spills from bikes, skateboards, roller skates, and other forms of locomotion. |

REMOVAL: *On fabric:*

1. Rub the affected area with ice, then use a dull knife or spoon to remove as much as possible.

2. Rub glycerin into the stain and lay stained area over an absorbent cloth. (If tar has dried, warm the glycerin first, then spread it over the stain.)

3. When the stain is softened, tap the back of it with an old toothbrush or spoon to remove as much tar as possible. Replace the cloth as necessary.

4. Rub eucalyptus oil or turpentine into the remaining stain and blot. Continue until you have removed as much stain as possible.

5. Apply laundry presoak (spot stain remover) and let stand several minutes.

6. Launder according to garment label.

7. If the stain remains, rub liquid laundry detergent into the stain and rub it between your thumbs.

8. Rinse well in hot water.

9. Repeat steps 7 and 8 until you have removed as much stain as possible.

10. If the stain remains, apply a laundry presoak (spot stain remover) and let stand several minutes.

11. Launder in the hottest water safe for the fabric.

12. If the stain remains, lay garment in the sun and sponge with a mild bleach, such as hydrogen peroxide. Keep stain moist.

13. Rinse well.

On carpet:

1. Rub the affected area with ice, then use a dull knife or spoon to remove as much as possible. If tar is dried, rub warm glycerin into it and let it soak until the tar or asphalt is softened.

2. Blot stain gently with an absorbent cloth to remove as much tar and asphalt as possible. Replace cloth as it becomes covered with the stain. Continue until you have removed as much stain as possible.

3. Sponge the stain with eucalyptus oil or turpentine, blotting continuously.

4. Sponge the stain with a sudsy detergent solution, then scrub with an old toothbrush to work solution into carpet.

5. Blot with water to rinse.

6. If the stain remains, apply dry-cleaning fluid or a carpet spotter according to manufacturer's directions.

WINDSHIELD WIPER FLUID

GENERAL DESCRIPTION:
Liquid stored in a container under an automobile's hood, which is shot onto the front window of the vehicle and then wiped off to clean the glass and increase visibility. Although water can be used in place of windshield wiper fluid in warm weather, the brightly colored fluid is still the best choice for this job—it contains detergent to clean the windshield, and antifreeze to prevent it from freezing in the reservoir or on the windshield.

SEASON:
Because it rains most often in springtime in most climates, there may be a decrease in the prevalence of this stain then. Similarly, since water can be used in place of wiper fluid during warm weather, there may be fewer stains in summer.

AREAS OF OCCURRENCE:
Windshield wiper fluid hardly ever stains when it is in use, because its use occurs outside the vehicle, but it is activated from inside—where you are protected by the windshield being cleaned. A stain will most likely occur as you fill the reservoir and the fluid splashes. Filling up the windshield wiper fluid in your car exposes gloves, scarves, and the sleeves and fronts of jackets and sweaters to the possibility of a stain.

REMOVAL: 1.   Rinse back of stain well with cold water or club soda.

2.   If the stain remains, rub with dishwashing liquid or liquid enzyme detergent. Let stand several minutes. (Do not use bar or natural soap of any kind on the fabric or the stain will set.)

3.   Rinse well with cold water.

4.   Launder according to garment label.

5.   If the stain remains, rub it with liquid enzyme detergent, then soak and agitate in cold water for 30 minutes or until the stain is removed.

6.   Rinse well.

7.   Apply laundry presoak (spot stain remover) and let stand several minutes.

8.   Launder according to garment label.

BODILY
FUNCTIONS

BLOOD

GENERAL
DESCRIPTION:

A bodily fluid in human beings and other vertebrates, which circulates oxygen and nutrients throughout the body and transports waste away from the cells. Human blood consists of red blood cells, white blood cells, and platelets suspended in plasma. Blood is necessary for life, but you can lose more than half of it and survive (though you'll be in very bad shape). In the second it takes to turn the page of this book, about two million of your red blood cells will die. During that same period, your bone marrow will have produced the same number of new ones.

SEASON:

Unfortunately, bloodstains are not limited by season. Humans run the risk of stains from this precious fluid at every turn, in cases of accidental scrapes, cuts, and scratches. There are a few times of year when bloodstains may be more prevalent—for instance, during hunting seasons, when the blood that does the staining belongs to an animal that falls prey to the hunter's wiles. Anyone who has a period knows to guard against bloodstains for about one week each month. And some, like doctors, nurses, workers in meat-packing plants, and people who think they're vampires, must be vigilant every day of the year.

AREAS OF
OCCURRENCE:

Blood can reach any area of any garment, and sometimes even furniture or carpeting. Especially vulnerable places include the knees and elbows of children's clothes, as scrapes are common in these areas; the ankle area of socks, where blisters often occur; undergarments; sheets; the seats of chairs; and white skirts or pants (as they seem to attract the stuff).

TIME OF OCCURRENCE: Bloodstains can happen at any time of day or night, but stains resulting from malicious acts are more likely to occur at night, in dark alleys and places better left unvisited. Benign stains caused by cuts and scrapes, as well as from menstruation, occur year-round.

VARIATIONS OF SIGNIFICANCE: Raw meat

REMOVAL: *On fabric:*

1. Rinse the stain immediately and thoroughly with cold saltwater. Do not use hot water or the stain will set. For dried stains, soak in cold saltwater up to 30 minutes or until the stain is loosened.

2. If stain remains, soak in a mixture of liquid enzyme detergent and cold water for up to 30 minutes.

3. Rinse well.

4. If stain remains, moisten cornstarch, baking soda, or unseasoned meat tenderizer and rub it into the stain to absorb some of the blood. Let the fabric dry in direct sunlight to further bleach the stain.

5. Brush the powder off once the garment is fully dry.

6. Rinse well with cold water.

7. Apply laundry presoak (spot stain remover) to any remaining stain and let stand several minutes.

8. Launder with liquid enzyme detergent.

On carpet:

1. Use a dull knife or spoon to remove as much as possible.

2. Blot remaining liquid with an absorbent cloth.

3. Sponge the stain with a sudsy mixture of liquid enzyme detergent and cold water, then sponge with cold, clean water. Repeat until you have removed as much stain as possible.

4. If the stain remains, sponge with a mild bleach, such as lemon juice or hydrogen peroxide (do not saturate carpet) then sponge with cold clear water. Repeat as needed.

5. If the stain remains, treat with a carpet spotter according to manufacturer's directions.

EXCREMENT

GENERAL DESCRIPTION: Waste matter, especially solid waste, discharged from the body. There's no getting around the fact that most people turn up their noses at excrement. Even though it comes from the body and is natural, it's just not terribly pleasant stuff. Many people are used to dodging doggie-doo on the sidewalks, but as bad as it might be in your area, it probably used to be worse. Before 1978, when New York City enacted a "pooper scooper" law that made it mandatory for dog owners to pick up after their pets, the city streets were weathering almost 500,000 pounds of pooch waste a day.

SEASON: 	Since both people and animals must empty their bowels regularly, even daily, excrement stains can occur any time of year.
AREAS OF OCCURRENCE:	During an accident, a person can embarrassingly stain their own undergarments, trousers, or bed linens. When changing a baby or cleaning out the litter box, those who neglect to roll up their sleeves beforehand may fall victim to this particularly nasty stain. The same goes for cleaning up after Rover in the park. In some instances, the act of cleaning up a pet's or child's excrement might result in stains on the fronts of jackets or sweaters, but these will hopefully be rare.
TIME OF OCCURRENCE:	Since adults do not soil themselves as a matter of course, this sort of stain is unpredictable, though no time is completely off the table. New parents can testify that during the first months of a baby's life, there is absolutely no hour of the day or night that is without risk of catastrophic excrement experiences. Early morning or late night are the most common hours for incurring a stain while cleaning up after a pet or changing a baby, since grogginess may undermine vigilance during these times.

REMOVAL:

1. Use a dull knife or spoon to remove as much as possible.

2. For fresh stains, soak and agitate the fabric thoroughly in cold water. For dried stains, soak fabric in a soapy mixture of cold water and liquid enzyme detergent for 30 minutes or until the stain is loosened. Rinse well.

3. If the stain remains, rub a liquid enzyme detergent into the stain and let stand several minutes.

4. Launder according to garment label.

5. If the stain remains, soak in an enzyme detergent mixture and cold water mixture up to 30 minutes.

6. Rinse well.

7. Apply a laundry presoak (spot stain remover) and launder again. On white fabrics, especially baby clothes, bleach any remaining stain by blotting with lemon juice and setting to dry in the sun.

RING AROUND THE COLLAR

GENERAL DESCRIPTION: A buildup of sweat and dirt on the part of a shirt, coat, dress, blouse, or jacket that touches the neck. This pesky laundry problem gets worse the longer it sits. When ring around the collar is noticed, it should be taken care of as soon as possible. This stain came into the spotlight in the 1970s; Wisk detergent had a successful advertising campaign at that time, promising to eradicate ring around the collar when applied directly to shirts and blouses before laundering.

SEASON: Summer is a time when this stain is probably more common, as sweat is the main ingredient of ring around the collar. However, since collared, button-down dress shirts are worn throughout the year with suits and jackets, this stain will appear throughout the year.

<table>
<tr><td>

AREAS OF
OCCURRENCE:

</td><td>

As the name indicates, this stain is found only on the collars and necklines of garments. If you have ring around the collar on your trousers, socks, bedsheets, or (somehow) carpets, what you have is ring around the trousers, ring around the socks, and so forth.

</td></tr>
</table>

AREAS OF OCCURRENCE:

As the name indicates, this stain is found only on the collars and necklines of garments. If you have ring around the collar on your trousers, socks, bedsheets, or (somehow) carpets, what you have is ring around the trousers, ring around the socks, and so forth.

TIME OF OCCURRENCE:

This stain is caused by buildup, so the time of incurring the stain is largely indeterminate. You are likely to notice the stain in the evening, after five o'clock, when changing out of office garb and into loungewear.

REMOVAL:

1. Scrub collar with liquid laundry detergent. Let stand several minutes.

 2. Launder in the hottest water safe for the fabric.

3. If the stain remains, let air dry and repeat steps 1 and 2. For particularly stubborn stains, apply a laundry presoak (spot stain remover) and launder again.

SEMEN

GENERAL DESCRIPTION:

A whitish fluid produced in the testicles, containing sperm cells. On average, a person who produces semen will generate 14 gallons of it over a lifetime, yet American families include less than one child on average. This implies quite a bit of semen that does not reach its destination, which in turn implies quite a few stained sheets.

SEASON:

Semen knows no season—humans are always ready to reproduce. Risk of staining increases, however, around the fourteenth of February each year, as well as during the time "spring fever," which is epidemic, strikes.

AREAS OF
OCCURRENCE:

Sheets, pants, underwear, and towels are common places to find this stain, but it is possible for semen to wind up on any piece of clothing after being swept up in the moment. Semen has been discovered as far from the mark as the floor, a T-shirt, a pajama top, a dress, the pillowcase, even a curtain, following extreme carelessness.

TIME OF
OCCURRENCE:

This stain may occur at any time, but early morning and late night are standard. Stains are usually found in the morning, either because they've just occurred, or because daylight exposes evidence from last night's activities.

REMOVAL:

1. Hold fabric stain side down under cold running water to force water through fabric.

2. Soak and agitate the fabric in cold water until loosened.

3. If the stain remains, rub liquid laundry detergent into the stain and let stand several minutes.

4. Launder according to garment label.

SWEAT

GENERAL
DESCRIPTION:

The moisture exuded from the body during strenuous activity; perspiration. This is one stain that every human being encounters at least once in their lifetime. It is truly universal, and it is one of the most irritating stains worldwide. While not typically subject to stains from this fluid, other animals most certainly sweat. Though the average person sweats two and a half quarts every day, it is nothing when compared with the camel. These humped creatures lose up to 30 percent of their body weight in perspiration and still function. Most mammals would die after sweating out just 15 percent of their weight.

SEASON:

Since the body perspires when it needs to cool down, sweat stains aren't limited to a particular time of year, but the risk is much greater during summer months when every article of clothing, no matter how lightweight, is likely to be profusely sweated upon. During the winter cold-and-flu season, with its fevers and heavy blankets, sweat stains may also spike.

AREAS OF OCCURRENCE:

Undoubtedly the most common spot for a sweat stain is the armpit areas of T-shirts, turtlenecks, blouses, and dresses. This stain is the worst because the area is subject to much repeat staining, making the yellowing of the fabric there especially nasty. All pieces of workout clothing are subject to this stain, particularly T-shirts, tank tops, and sports bras. In the summer, bed linens are susceptible to this stain, especially in locales requiring air-conditioning.

REMOVAL:

1. Sponge the stain with ammonia or white vinegar. For heavy stains, rub with liquid laundry detergent and soak, occasionally rubbing stain between thumbs, until loosened.

2. Rinse well.

3. Repeat steps 1 and 2 until no more stain can be removed.

4. If the stain remains, apply laundry presoak (spot stain remover) and let stand several minutes.

5. Launder with a bleach that is safe for the fabric.

URINE

GENERAL
DESCRIPTION:

Liquid waste matter excreted by the kidneys, a byproduct of cellular metabolism. Urine stains are usually yellow and are always embarrassing. Whether the stain is made by an excited dog, a crying baby, or oneself when in a drunken stupor, it should be removed as soon as it occurs.

SEASON:

Urine stains can happen at any time, especially to young children and, consequently, their parents. There are particular times when adults might experience incontinence, namely during summer when the blockbuster comedic movies debut, and the extreme cold of winter, when blasts of air can be shocking in more than one way. Folks prone to drinking large amounts of alcohol might also find they experience troubling urine stains throughout the year.

AREAS OF
OCCURRENCE:

One's own urine stains are generally limited to a few areas, including underwear and the crotch areas of pants. Sheets are a likely target for small children, while babies may produce urine stains on their parents' waists, on furniture, and sometimes even on ceilings if their diapers are off. For babies, there is no escaping this stain—all garments are at risk.

TIME OF OCCURRENCE:	Urine stainings are most likely after 9 p.m., when the children are in bed, or much later, around 2 a.m., after the local pub closes.
REMOVAL:	*For fresh stains on fabric:*

1. Rinse well with cold water.

2. If the stain remains, mix a solution of 1 tablespoon ammonia in 1/2 cup warm water. Sponge the mixture over the stain and rinse well.

3. If the stain remains, apply a laundry presoak (spot stain remover) and let stand several minutes.

4. Launder according to garment label.

5. If the stain remains, dilute hydrogen peroxide with water at a ratio of 1 to 4. Sponge the dilution on the stain, then rinse well with warm water. Repeat as needed.

For dried stains on fabric:

1. Soak and agitate stain in cold water up to 1 hour.

2. Rub a liquid enzyme detergent into stain. Let stand several minutes. For persistent stains, rub with detergent, then soak in cold water for 30 minutes to 1 hour.

3. Launder according to garment label.

4. If the stain remains, launder with a bleach that is safe for the fabric. Test first for colorfastness.

On carpet:

1. Blot as much stain as possible with an absorbent cloth.

2. Sponge the stain with a sudsy mixture of cold water and liquid enzyme detergent. Scrub the stain with an old toothbrush and let stand for 15 to 20 minutes.

3. Sponge with a clean, damp cloth, then blot with a dry cloth.

4. Repeat steps 2 and 3 until no more stain can be removed.

5. Allow carpet to dry thoroughly. Direct a fan onto the stain, if possible.

6. If an odor remains, repeat steps 2 through 5.

7. Once odor is eliminated, apply a carpet spotter according to manufacturer's directions.

8. If the stain lightens the carpet, sponge with a mild solution of 1 teaspoon ammonia to 1 cup water to restore the color. Test first for colorfastness.

9. Sponge with a clean, damp cloth, then blot with a dry cloth.

VOMIT

GENERAL
DESCRIPTION: The substance that is forced from the stomach during regurgitation or throwing up, composed of whatever was recently ingested by the sufferer along with stom-

ach acids and juices. This stain is unique in that it can vary significantly according to its makeup, which changes depending on what the vomiter has lately consumed. Extreme fear of vomiting or seeing someone vomit is called emetophobia. American English has many slang and euphemistic terms for vomiting—among the more colorful are "praying to the porcelain god," "laughing at the carpet," and "Technicolor yawn," although you're likelier to hear about "booting," "hurling," "puking," and the classic "barfing."

SEASON:

This stain knows no season, as a night of too much drinking or a bite of rotten food that causes vomiting may take place any time of year. You might notice an increase in the occurrence of this stain during an outbreak of norovirus (most common in winter through early spring), when many sufferers are unable to keep anything in their stomachs.

AREAS OF
OCCURRENCE:

Pant legs and the fronts of blouses, sweaters, and jackets are particularly susceptible to this stain, especially when too much alcohol causes an upset stomach. Sickness from liquor will also render carpets and the walls of bathrooms vulnerable, as well as the cuffs of pants, and shoes and socks. (In fact, floors aren't safe from illness-based vomiting either, since feverish delirium can be just as bad as intoxication when it comes to directing or controlling a spew. Sick kids, especially, are a menace to carpets.) When food poisoning or a virus is what's making you sick, nightgowns, pajamas, and robes are particularly at risk. Either situation can cause stains on sheets, blankets, and pillowcases, so you should be careful when resting. The school year is a sickness-prone time for some college students who go to frat parties or formal dances, so fancy dresses and tuxedos, as well as any party clothes, are at risk then.

TIME OF OCCURRENCE: Throwing up is an activity that is not limited to a certain time of day, unfortunately. Depending on the vomiter's level of incoherence—whether caused by illness or alcohol—the resulting vomit stain may be more likely to occur during the wee hours of the night.

REMOVAL: *On fabric:*

1. Use a dull knife or spoon to remove as much as possible.

2. Flush the back of the stain well with cold water.

3. Dilute ammonia with warm water at a ratio of 1 to 4. Sponge the mixture into the stain.

4. Rinse well.

5. If the stain remains, soak in a sudsy mixture of liquid enzyme detergent and warm water until the stain is removed or up to 1 hour.

6. If the stain remains, apply laundry presoak (spot stain remover).

7. Launder according to garment label.

On carpet:

1. Use a dull knife or spoon to remove as much as possible.

2. Pour club soda on stain. Let stand several seconds.

3. Blot with an absorbent cloth. Replace cloth as it becomes saturated.

4. Repeat steps 2 and 3 as needed.

5. If the stain remains, treat with a carpet spotter according to manufacturer's directions.

BATHROOM
and BEAUTY
PRODUCTS

BABY OIL

GENERAL DESCRIPTION: Nontoxic oil, usually mineral oil, which maintains its clear color regardless of temperature and often has a pleasant scent. Baby oil is a favorite of parents everywhere for its use as a skin-softening agent for babies and adults alike. It is appreciated by others, too, including bodybuilders, admirers of the sun, and makeup artists who want their subjects to have the appearance of a sweaty glow.

SEASON:

Though babies are generated constantly, baby-oil stains increase during the sunny summer months, when devoted sun-worshippers slather themselves with the stuff while striving for the perfect tan.

AREAS OF OCCURRENCE

The area affected by a baby oil stain depends on how you employ the oil. When used to keep a baby's skin supple, it might stain baby's clothes or blankets. When used to enhance the effects of the sun's rays, it might stain bathing suits, towels, shorts, or sundresses. And when used by a bodybuilder to draw attention to shining muscles, Speedos or string bikinis may bear the stain.

REMOVAL:
1. Use a dull knife or spoon to remove as much as possible.

2. Blot remaining liquid with an absorbent cloth.

3. Sprinkle salt, baking soda, cornstarch, or talcum powder on stain to absorb excess oil and let stand 10 to 15 minutes, then brush off.

4. Rub colorless dishwashing liquid into stain. Let stand 1 to 2 minutes.

5. Soak in a sudsy mixture of hot water and dishwashing liquid for up to 30 minutes.

6. Rinse the back of the stain well with hot water.

7. Use a dull knife or spoon again to remove any loosened oil from the fabric.

8. If the stain remains, make a paste of baking soda and water at a ratio of approximately 3 to 1, spread on stain and let dry, then brush off.

9. Apply laundry presoak (spot stain remover) and let stand several minutes to penetrate fabric.

10. Launder in the hottest water safe for the fabric. For extra-heavy stains, replace half the amount of detergent with baking soda.

BLUSH OR ROUGE

GENERAL DESCRIPTION: Any of various red-tinted cosmetics used for coloring the cheeks. Since most people try to hide their embarrassment and are further embarrassed when caught in a scarlet blush, it seems odd that there is a desire to imitate this reaction. Odd or no, people have been artificially reddening their cheeks for centuries. The Romans used vermilion (powdered mercury sulfide) to paint the faces of military heroes. In the Middle Ages and Renaissance Europe, cosmetics contained artificial vermilion, made by combining mercury and sulfur. This was not any less toxic.

SEASON: ❄	This is one of the few cosmetics that is typically seasonal, because its application may be discontinued during summer, when the sun lends a natural pink glow to the cheeks. Winter may therefore be a more likely time to find this stain. Those involved with theater, however, will probably incur this stain year-round, as stage lights wash out even the pinkest faces.
AREAS OF OCCURRENCE:	Blush and rouge stains can appear almost anywhere, depending upon whether it is your own blush or another party's that is responsible for the staining. Your own blush is likely to show itself on the collar or front of your blouse or jacket, or on your coat or scarf, as the weather becomes colder. Another's blush could appear on the front of a dress shirt, or on a necktie. During opening night at the theater or anytime during the run of a production, rouge can find its way onto any article of an actor's clothing, due to quick changes in the wings.
TIME OF OCCURRENCE:	When the blush in question is your own, the stain will usually appear as a stain during application—in the morning before work or in the evening before a date. If another person's blush is to blame for the stain, it was most likely achieved during a romantic encounter—usually in the evening.
REMOVAL:	I. Use a dull knife or spoon to remove as much as possible.
SOAP	2. Dampen stain and rub with bar soap, dishwashing liquid, or liquid laundry detergent. Rub the stain between thumbs.
⬭	3. Rinse well.

4. Repeat steps 2 and 3 until no more stain can be removed.

5. If the stain remains, especially if makeup is oily, soak in a sudsy mixture of water and detergent for 10 to 15 minutes.

6. Rinse well.

7. If the stain remains, treat with a laundry presoak (spot stain remover).

8. Launder according to garment label.

DEODORANTS OR ANTIPERSPIRANTS

GENERAL DESCRIPTION: Substances used to inhibit or mask perspiration or other causes of bodily odors; deodorants reduce or cover up the smells caused by the bacterial breakdown of perspiration, and antiperspirants prevent sweating altogether. Sweat itself is odorless, but the normal bacteria found on human skin break it down into smelly compounds. For this reason, in many cultures adults apply deodorants and antiperspirants to their armpits to prevent excessive sweat and odor. These substances are available in many forms, including roll-on liquids, sprays, gels, solids, powders, and in some cases, even natural crystals. In a pinch, chamomile tea or rosemary can be used as effective deodorants. Wet the tea bag or the herb, and rub it on the offending areas. If possible, leave in place for a few minutes.

| SEASON: | Perspiration, and thus staining from deodorants and antiperspirants, occurs all year long, but it is much more prevalent during the balmy summer months, when the use of deodorant is demanded. |

| AREAS OF OCCURRENCE: | Stains from deodorants and antiperspirants will be found not only in the armpit areas of clothes, but also on the sides and waist areas of pull-over shirts or dresses. In the summer there is also a chance that such stains will mysteriously materialize on other areas of clothing, for instance the backs or shoulders of T-shirts and dresses, especially after cuddling with a freshly showered and groomed loved one. |

| TIME OF OCCURRENCE: | Antiperspirant and deodorant stains are two of the most opportunistic—they tend to present themselves at the least advantageous times, such as just before work, in the moments leading up to a blind date, and other times when grooming is rushed and of the utmost importance. |

REMOVAL: *For fresh stains on fabric:*

1. Mix a laundry presoak (spot stain remover) with lukewarm water and sponge on the dry fabric stain. Let stand several minutes.

2. Rinse well.

3. Repeat steps 1 and 2 until no more stain can be removed.

4. If the stain damages color, restore it by sponging the damaged area with ammonia. If treating wool or silk for a stain, dilute ammonia with an equal amount of water.

5. Rinse well.

6. Launder in the hottest water safe for the fabric.

For dried stains on fabric:

1. Mix a laundry presoak (spot stain remover) and lukewarm water. Place stain facedown on an absorbent cloth and sponge the back of it with the mixture. Let stand several minutes.

2. Rinse well. Repeat until no more stain can be removed.

3. Rub liquid enzyme detergent into the stain.

4. Launder in the hottest water safe for the fabric.

5. If fabric has discolored, restore by blotting with white vinegar.

6. Rinse well.

EYELINER OR EYE SHADOW

GENERAL DESCRIPTION: EYELINER: **A cosmetic applied along the eyelash line to accentuate the eyes.** EYE SHADOW: **A cosmetic coloring material, usually a powder or cream, applied to the eyelids.** Eye makeup has gone through many changes in its long history. Ancient Egyptians used crushed malachite, a green semiprecious stone, in their cosmetics. Nowadays, synthetic materials are used to make both eyeliner and shadow, and the styles are endless. From cat-eye liner in the 1960s to blue shadow up to the brows in the 1980s to having liner permanently tattooed on the lids in the twenty-first century, eyeliner and shadow have offered centuries of value to people who want to enhance their upper face.

SEASON: Eye makeup knows no season, though the colors worn during summer may differ from those worn in winter.

AREAS OF OCCURRENCE: Perhaps the most common—and certainly the most irritating—occurrence of this stain happens not when applying either substance, but when shadow or liner opens or breaks in a handbag or suitcase. This results in stains not only on the lining of the bag, but on any items in close proximity to the cosmetic. Of course, sloppiness with shadow or liner may result in stains to sleeves or fronts of blouses or dresses as well.

TIME OF OCCURRENCE: Any time makeup needs a touch-up is a time for this stain to occur, but more likely times are the morning before work or the evening before a date, when you are perfecting the beauty ritual.

REMOVAL:
1. Use a dull knife or spoon to remove as much as possible.

[SOAP] 2. Dampen stain and rub with bar soap, dishwashing liquid, or liquid laundry detergent. Rub the stain between thumbs.

3. Rinse well.

4. Repeat steps 2 and 3 until no more stain can be removed.

5. If the stain remains, especially if makeup is oily, soak in a sudsy mixture of water and detergent for 10 to 15 minutes.

6. Rinse well.

7. If the stain remains, treat with a laundry presoak (spot stain remover).

8. Launder according to garment label.

FOUNDATION

GENERAL DESCRIPTION: A cosmetic, usually in cream or liquid form, that is used as a base for facial makeup. Foundation smooths the tone and texture of the skin and reduces pore visibility. It comes in a variety of forms, including powder, liquid, pan, and stick, with the latter three being the most likely to cause staining. Most people wear foundation only on their faces, though some, especially those involved in the theater, movies, or the television industry, wear it on their necks and chests as well.

SEASON: Foundation stains are seen more often in winter, when tans have faded and people are inclined to use more makeup to deepen the color of their skin. However, if foundation is worn in summer, the heat and perspiration may cause it to run, making a stain very likely.

AREAS OF OCCURRENCE: Foundation stains are found on the collars of shirts and dresses, but may also be found on pants, skirts, carpets, and towels, if dropped or spilled. A foundation stain is not limited to the makeup wearer's attire—it might present itself on collars, shoulders, chests, and lap areas that have been rested on by a foundationed face. Bed linens are another high-risk area, especially when you are in too big a hurry to wash your face before going to bed.

TIME OF OCCURRENCE:	Stains from foundation may occur in the hours before or during a night on the town, as foundation is sometimes applied more heavily later in the day. Some choose to wear foundation at work, so another prime time for stains is in the early morning.
REMOVAL:	1. Use a dull knife or spoon to remove as much as possible.
[SOAP]	2. Dampen stain and rub with bar soap, dishwashing liquid, or liquid laundry detergent. Rub the stain between thumbs.
◊	3. Rinse well.
	4. Repeat steps 2 and 3 until no more stain can be removed.
	5. If the stain remains, especially if makeup is oily, soak in a sudsy mixture of water and detergent for 10 to 15 minutes.
◊	6. Rinse well.
	7. If the stain remains, treat with a laundry presoak (spot stain remover).
♡	8. Launder according to garment label.

LIP BALM

GENERAL DESCRIPTION:	An oil-based substance used to moisturize the lips to keep them from becoming chapped or dry. The skin of the lips is much thinner than other skin and has no oil or sweat glands. Lips may also have less melanin, the natural pigment in skin that helps block the sun's

harmful ultraviolet rays. Because of these properties, lips tend to dry out very quickly—weather and other factors often help speed up this process—which leaves many people with the annoyance of chapped lips. Although "lip balm addiction" has become a popular myth, industry experts assert that there is no addictive ingredient in lip balm. No resistance builds up and no withdrawal symptoms occur if you choose to stop using lip balm.

SEASON:

Due to the increase in painful chapping of lips during the cold dry months of the year, lip balm stains are twice as likely to occur during winter. Any time you are sick with a cold or flu is a time this stain might appear, also due to increased chapping.

AREAS OF
OCCURRENCE:

Lip balm is invariably put away without its cap, or with its cap loosely applied, which ensures a lip balm stain on the insides of jacket and trouser pockets, as well as the linings of purses and backpacks. Individuals confined to bed with a cold may cause these stains on pillowcases or sheets, too.

TIME OF
OCCURRENCE:

Since lip balm is applied and reapplied throughout the day, there is rarely immunity to this stain, no matter what time of day.

REMOVAL:

1. Use a dull knife or spoon to remove as much as possible.

2. Dampen stain and rub with bar soap, dishwashing liquid, or liquid laundry detergent. Rub the stain between thumbs.

3. Rinse well.

4. Repeat steps 2 and 3 until no more stain can be removed.

5. If the stain remains, especially if makeup is oily, soak in a sudsy mixture of water and detergent for 10 to 15 minutes.

6. Rinse well.

7. If the stain remains, treat with a laundry presoak (spot stain remover).

8. Launder according to garment label.

LIPSTICK

GENERAL
DESCRIPTION:
A waxy cosmetic in stick form used to color the lips. Made from wax, oil, pearl essence (the silvery substance in the scales of herring and other fishes), dyes, and fragrances, lipstick has evolved as an essential part of the modern beauty toolkit.

SEASON:

This substance knows no season; any time is a good time to make your lips look important. Intense colors with tan hues are more often used in colder months, while paler, pastel shades are worn during spring and summer.

AREAS OF
OCCURRENCE:

Lipstick stains can appear almost anywhere. Your own lipstick is likely to show itself on the sleeves of your blouse or jacket, especially if no napkins are handy at dinner. The lipstick from another may appear on your collar, the front of a dress shirt, or a necktie. Sometimes a lipstick tube will get into the laundry, and once in the dryer, it melts and stains all garments with which it comes in contact.

VARIATIONS OF SIGNIFICANCE: Lip balm; lip gloss; lip liner; lipstick sealers

REMOVAL:
1. Use a dull knife or spoon to remove as much as possible.

2. Dampen stain and rub with bar soap, dishwashing liquid, or liquid laundry detergent. Rub the stain between thumbs.

3. Rinse well.

4. Repeat steps 2 and 3 until no more stain can be removed.

5. If the stain remains, especially if makeup is oily, soak in a sudsy mixture of water and detergent for 10 to 15 minutes.

6. Rinse well.

7. If the stain remains, treat with a laundry presoak (spot stain remover).

8. Launder according to garment label.

LOTION, HAND, BODY, OR SUNTAN

GENERAL DESCRIPTION: A liquid that is externally applied to the face, hands, or body for the purposes of soothing, moisturizing, or softening the skin, or (in the case of suntan lotion and face lotions with SPF) offering protection against ultraviolet light. As Earth's atmosphere continues to change, lotion may be one of our best protectors against the sun's damaging rays.

SEASON: Lotion stains are widespread in winter, when an overwhelming number of people are battling dry skin. This is not to say that a stain is not possible at other times of year—suntan lotion certainly takes its toll in stains during the summer. Professionals who require frequent hand-washing, like nurses, doctors, homemakers, and restaurant workers (especially in the kitchen), will suffer lotion stains year-round.

AREAS OF OCCURRENCE: Lotion stains appear everywhere as lotion can be—and is—used on all parts of the body. Since lotioned-up hands are slippery, it's also dismayingly easy to drop an entire bottle on your bathroom or bedroom floor.

VARIATIONS OF SIGNIFICANCE: Tissues coated with lotion

REMOVAL: *On fabric:*

1. Use a dull knife or spoon to remove as much as possible.

2. Blot remaining liquid with an absorbent cloth.

 3. Sprinkle salt, baking soda, cornstarch, or talcum powder on stain to absorb excess oil and let stand 10 to 15 minutes, then brush off.

4. Rub colorless dishwashing liquid into stain. Let stand 1 to 2 minutes.

5. Soak in a sudsy mixture of hot water and dishwashing detergent for up to 30 minutes.

6. Rinse the back of the stain well with hot water.

7. Use a dull knife or spoon again to remove any loosened lotion from the fabric.

8. If the stain remains, make a paste of baking soda and water at a ratio of approximately 3 to 1, spread on stain and let dry, then brush off.

9. Apply laundry presoak (spot stain remover) and let stand several minutes.

10. Launder in the hottest water safe for the fabric. For extra-heavy stains, replace half the amount of detergent with baking soda.

11. If the stain remains, repeat steps 3 through 10.

On carpet:

1. Use a dull knife or spoon to remove as much as possible.

2. Blot remaining liquid with an absorbent cloth. (For heavy or dark stains, it is best to call a professional cleaner.)

3. Sprinkle the stain with an absorbent powder, such as baking soda, cornstarch, cornmeal, or talcum powder. Let sit for 6 to 12 hours, then vacuum—do not brush the powder.

or

Spray with shaving cream and work into the carpet with an old toothbrush. Wipe with a damp cloth, then sponge with cold water.

or

> Dampen with club soda and blot with an absorbent cloth. Repeat as needed.

4. If the stain remains, apply dry-cleaning fluid (be careful not to wet the carpet backing with it) then sponge the stain with a damp cloth.

or

> Treat with a carpet spotter according to manufacturer's directions.

MASCARA

GENERAL DESCRIPTION:
A cosmetic applied to the eyelashes, usually with a bristled wand, to make them appear darker, longer, or fuller. Blue mascara enjoyed a brief popularity in the 1980s, white mascara resurfaces occasionally as a fashion-forward trend, and what would Halloween be without silver and gold? In the nineties there was even a brief vogue for "hair mascara"—thin streaks of temporary color applied to the hair. But despite innovations in color, application, and form (like "tubing mascara," which encases the lashes in tiny polymer tubes), most eye makeup wearers opt for basic black and brown, maybe in a waterproof formulation if they're the crying type.

SEASON:

Mascara is a year-round cosmetic, though the warmer months of summer may cause even the most expensive mascara to melt and run down the face and onto clothing while undressing.

AREAS OF OCCURRENCE:

The area underneath the eyes is without a doubt the most common staining ground for mascara; luckily, soap and water will generally remove this stain with no permanent damage. Watch for this stain on the sleeves of blouses and jackets, especially at the end of a grueling day when the eyes simply had to be rubbed. The insides of camisoles, shirts, and dresses are vulnerable to this stain when they are hastily removed. Of course, sheets, pillows, and nightgowns are most at risk for mascara stainings if nighttime makeup removal is neglected.

TIME OF OCCURRENCE:

Late-night hours are the most common for this stain, as exhaustion from a long day makes for careless rubbing of eyes and hasty removal of clothing. Early morning, before work, and evening, before a date, are also times when this stain may present itself, especially when you are short on preparation time.

REMOVAL:

1. Use a dull knife or spoon to remove as much as possible.

2. Dampen stain and rub with bar soap, dishwashing liquid, or liquid laundry detergent. Rub the stain between thumbs.

3. Rinse well.

4. Repeat steps 2 and 3 until no more stain can be removed.

5. If the stain remains, especially if makeup is oily, soak in a sudsy mixture of water and detergent for 10 to 15 minutes.

6. Rinse well.

7. If the stain remains, treat with a laundry presoak (spot stain remover).

8. Launder according to garment label.

NAIL POLISH

GENERAL DESCRIPTION:
A lacquer used to color or protect the fingernails or toenails. Fingernail polish often contains four or five chemicals the U.S. Environmental Protection Agency calls potentially harmful. Nail polish is considered a class 3 hazardous material (flammable liquid), and there are laws about how much nail polish you're allowed to transport by air in the United States.

SEASON:
Fashionable types may apply nail polish at all times of year, especially when special occasions are on the agenda. However, during the warm months of spring and summer, when sandals are standard attire and pedicures are as regularly sought as manicures, the chances of acquiring this stain double.

AREAS OF OCCURRENCE:
Nail polish stains can be found anywhere if hands or feet are used too soon after application. These stains are standard on socks, gloves, pants, and stockings. Bedsheets and towels are possible stain sites as well.

TIME OF OCCURRENCE:
Nail polish stains can happen any time a person has time for pampering, be it early in the morning or while watching television sitcoms in the evening.

REMOVAL:
On fabric:

1. Place the garment over an absorbent cloth and blot with an acetone nail polish remover. Straight

acetone can also be used; it is stronger and may work faster than nail polish remover. For either method, test first for colorfastness. If color is affected, substitute white vinegar for the nail polish remover. Apply slowly and blot continuously. Replace the cloth as it becomes saturated.

2. Rinse well.

3. Repeat steps 1 and 2 until you have removed as much stain as possible.

4. Apply a laundry presoak (spot stain remover) and let stand several minutes.

5. Launder according to garment label.

6. Let fabric dry in the sun after each washing, for added bleaching. For white or colorfast materials, try blotting the stain with a solution of equal parts white vinegar or hydrogen peroxide and water, then setting fabric in sunlight. Keep stain moist with solution until the stain is removed. If all else fails, launder with a bleach that is safe for the fabric. Test first for colorfastness.

On carpet:

1. Blot stain with an acetone nail polish remover. Straight acetone can also be used; it is stronger and may work faster than nail polish remover. For either method, test first for colorfastness. If color is affected, substitute white vinegar for the nail polish remover. Apply slowly and blot continuously. Blot well with clean water. Repeat until you have removed as much stain as possible.

2. If the stain remains, treat with a carpet spotter.

△ 3. Lighten the stain with a mild bleach, such as hydrogen peroxide, white vinegar, or lemon juice.

OINTMENT

<table>
<tr>
<td>GENERAL
DESCRIPTION:</td>
<td>A thick oil designed to externally deliver medicine or other active ingredients to the skin. Ointments, sometimes called salves or balms, are applied to the skin to treat a variety of ailments, including bug bites, chafing, swollen tissue, and many other socially unmentionable dilemmas. Their use can bring relief from these afflictions but can also create embarrassing stains.</td>
</tr>
<tr>
<td>SEASON:
</td>
<td>Ointments have uses in all seasons—in summer, it might be for cuts, scrapes, rashes, or arthritic joints agitated by athletic use; in winter, as a cure for dry or irritated skin, and as a medication to soothe coughs. Diaper rash, a seasonless ailment for young children, calls for treatment with ointments and vigilance against their stains.</td>
</tr>
<tr>
<td>AREAS OF
OCCURRENCE:
</td>
<td>Ointment is not limited to a particular area of use and therefore its stains can be anywhere. Some commonly affected areas include pajama tops, athletic uniforms, undergarments, the elbow areas of sweatshirts and long-sleeved jerseys, the knee areas of pants and stockings, cloth diapers, and bed linens.</td>
</tr>
<tr>
<td>REMOVAL:</td>
<td>1. Use a dull knife or spoon to remove as much as possible.</td>
</tr>
</table>

2. Blot remaining stain with an absorbent cloth.

3. Sprinkle salt, baking soda, cornstarch, or talcum powder on stain to absorb excess ointment and let stand 10 to 15 minutes, then brush off.

4. Rub colorless dishwashing liquid into stain. Let stand 1 to 2 minutes.

5. Soak in a sudsy mixture of hot water and dishwashing liquid for up to 30 minutes.

6. Rinse the back of the stain well with hot water.

7. Use a dull knife or spoon to remove any loosened ointment from the fabric.

8. If the stain remains, make a paste of baking soda and water at a ratio of approximately 3 to 1, spread on stain and let dry, then brush off.

9. Apply laundry presoak (spot stain remover) and let stand several minutes to penetrate fabric.

10. Launder in the hottest water safe for the fabric. For extra-heavy stains, replace half the amount of detergent with baking soda.

On carpet:

1. Use a dull knife or spoon to remove as much as possible.

2. Blot remaining liquid with an absorbent cloth. (For heavy or dark stains, it is best to call a professional cleaner.)

3. Sprinkle the stain with an absorbent powder, such as baking soda, cornstarch, cornmeal, or talcum powder. Let sit for 6 to 12 hours, then vacuum (do not brush) the powder.

or

Spray with shaving cream and work into the carpet with an old toothbrush. Wipe with a damp cloth, then sponge with cold water.

or

Dampen with club soda and blot gently. Repeat as needed.

4. If the stain remains, apply dry-cleaning fluid (be careful not to wet the carpet backing with it), then sponge the stain with a damp cloth.

or

Treat with a carpet spotter according to manufacturer's directions.

PERFUME

GENERAL DESCRIPTION: A mixture of natural or synthetic aromatic compounds in a solvent (usually ethanol), which can be sprayed or splashed on skin, clothing, or surfaces to impart a pleasant smell. The conquest of Alexander the Great in the fourth century B.C. first brought perfume to Greece, and since that time, it has been a vital ingredient in the mating rituals of humans. Many people believe that scent is extremely important in attracting potential mates, basing their belief on the known allure of both formulated perfumes as well as the body's natural perfumes, called pheromones. Perfume has a long history of helping to woo; legend has it that when setting out to meet Marc Antony, Cleopatra put perfume on the sails of her barge.

SEASON:

Both men and women like to smell good regardless of season, making perfume a year-round stain. The heat of summer sometimes facilitates the transfer of perfume from skin to clothing, so this stain may be a bit more common at this time of year.

AREAS OF
OCCURRENCE:

Perfume most frequently stains the cuffs and collars or neck areas of button-down blouses, dresses, and suit jackets. However, those who use perfume adventurously might find stains in such out-of-the-way spots as behind the knees of trousers, or on lacy undergarments. Unfortunately, as scents are generally packaged in glass bottles, there is a high incidence of breakage when these bottles are transported in pocketbooks or luggage. When this occurs, the linings of bags as well as any clothing that may be in the vicinity are affected.

REMOVAL:

1. Rinse back of stain well with cold water or club soda.

2. If the stain remains, rub with dishwashing liquid or liquid enzyme detergent. Let stand several minutes. Do not use bar or natural soap of any kind on the fabric or the stain will set.

3. Rinse well with cold water.

4. Launder according to garment label.

5. If the stain remains, rub it with liquid enzyme detergent, then soak and agitate in cold water for 30 minutes, or until the stain is removed.

6. Rinse well.

7. Apply laundry presoak (spot stain remover) and let stand several minutes.

8. Launder according to garment label.

TOOTHPASTE

GENERAL
DESCRIPTION:
A dentifrice (tooth-cleaning agent) in gel or paste form, generally spread onto the teeth with a specialized brush. Toothpaste was invented by the ancient Egyptians; one recipe from the fourth century A.D. included salt, pepper, mint, and dried iris, and an Austrian dentist who tried it in 2003 said it made his gums bleed. These days, toothpaste is high tech. Not only does it come in an array of different containers—from flip-caps to complicated canisters—there are also different types that boast a variety of uses. Some include both paste and a gel, each serving a unique function; there are tartar control pastes, pastes that include mouthwash, whitening pastes, and pastes that are said to freshen the "whole mouth." Regardless of your preferred paste, a toothbrush, toothpaste, and dental floss are the necessary ingredients for overall dental hygiene.

SEASON:	Teeth need brushing year-round; there is no season for higher risk of obtaining a toothpaste stain.
AREAS OF OCCURRENCE:	The fronts of pajamas, nightgowns, and robes are particularly vulnerable to this stain, especially when you are groggy in the morning or just before bedtime. Toothpaste stains are often incurred on the fronts of blouses, jackets, and dresses, especially when you are hurried while getting ready to go out.
TIME OF OCCURRENCE:	Early in the morning before work and in the evening before going out for dinner or dancing are especially irksome times to experience this stain, because it often requires a costume change. Late at night before bed is another stain-prone time; the probability of a stain increases exponentially as the level of exhaustion increases.

REMOVAL:

1. Use a dull knife or spoon to remove as much as possible.

2. Blot stain with a sudsy mixture of cold water and liquid enzyme detergent.

3. Rinse well. Repeat until no more stain can be removed.

4. Launder according to garment label.

OFFICE *and* SCHOOL PRODUCTS

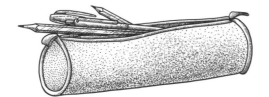

ADHESIVES OR STICKERS

ADHESIVE: **A sticky substance that is used to adhere two objects or surfaces together.** STICKER: **A piece of paper or other flat material with an adhesive backing.** Adhesives and stickers have become omnipresent. From the "inspected by" sticker in the pocket of a new pair of pants to the price tag on a loaf of bread to the transparent tape sealing a wrapped present, adhesives and stickers are literally everywhere. In addition to the more common uses, tape has been employed in some especially interesting places: pigeon breeders suggest using clear tape to hold cracked pigeon eggs together until they can hatch, but it's also been used as a protective shield on the Goodyear blimp and to repair a tear in the Declaration of Independence.

SEASON: The season for stains from adhesives and stickers is boundless—you are just as likely to suffer a stain from a "Hello, my name is" sticker on the lapel of a jacket in the winter months as from an errant piece of tape in the summer.

AREAS OF
OCCURRENCE: Stickers are maddening in their ability to stick undetected onto the back of a pant leg or to the hidden elbow of the arm on a shirt. Other areas where stains are found include the lapels of jackets and the upper chest region of sweaters, dresses, and blouses; anywhere a store might see fit to place a price sticker; the inside of a shirt, pants, or even a pocket, where inspectors place their stamp of approval; and the insides of garments worn over knees and elbows, where adhesive bandages have been used.

VARIATIONS OF SIGNIFICANCE:	Name tags; adhesive bandages; duct tape; gold stars; price stickers; packing tape

REMOVAL:

1. Rub an ice cube on the stain or place in the freezer. Use a dull knife or spoon to remove as much as possible.

2. Sponge the stain with eucalyptus oil, baby oil, or cooking oil until the stain is loosened. Use a dull knife or spoon to remove as much as possible.

3. Rinse well.

4. Repeat steps 2 and 3 until you've removed as much stain as possible.

5. Sponge the stain with a laundry presoak (spot stain remover).

6. Launder according to garment label.

7. If the stain remains, place it facedown on an absorbent cloth and apply dry-cleaning fluid to the back of the stain. Use the fluid according to manufacturer's directions. Let the stain dry.

8. Rinse thoroughly.

9. Launder according to garment label.

On glass or metal surfaces:

1. If adhesive is water-soluble, sponge with warm sudsy water or cover with a warm, wet cloth and let stand several minutes. If adhesive is solvent-based, sponge with nail polish remover or acetone until softened. Test first in an inconspicuous area.

2. Once softened, use a dull knife or spoon to remove as much as possible.

3. Repeat steps 1 and 2 as needed.

CARBON PAPER OR COPIER TONER

GENERAL DESCRIPTION:

CARBON PAPER: **A paper treated with carbon or other material, which when inserted between two sheets of regular paper will transfer any marks made on the upper sheet onto the lower one.** COPIER TONER: **A powder, either dry or suspended in liquid, used in photocopiers to produce an image on paper.** Though carbon paper is rarely used today (artists and dressmakers may still employ it), it has left its mark on future technology; the email function "cc" indicates that a "carbon copy" of the electronic image will be sent. Copier toner, however, is still used in office buildings around the globe and causes no small amount of trouble. Due to its powdery consistency as well as the largely enigmatic nature of copy machines, toner is very likely to make a mess.

SEASON:

Toner must be replaced in copy machines every few months, depending on the volume of work the machine handles, so these stains appear throughout the year.

AREAS OF OCCURRENCE:

Stains incurred from carbon paper are most likely to be on the fingers and hands of the person using it; the most common way a stain will appear is when you rub the affected area on clothing. Pants, jackets, and dress shirts are also likely victims of this stain. Toner, however, is far wilier, and its stains often appear on shoes, socks, the bottoms of pant legs, carpeting, and any other fabric unlucky enough to be in the path of the toner cartridge.

TIME OF OCCURRENCE: It is unlikely that stains from these products will be incurred at any time of day other than between the hours of 9 a.m. and 5 p.m., when offices are in full swing.

REMOVAL:

1. Shake off as much loose powder as possible. Hold the garment over the sink and tap the back of the stain lightly with an old toothbrush to help remove powder.

2. Brush the stain carefully with the toothbrush. Do not touch the stain with your hand; the oil on your skin will spread the stain.

3. Sponge the stain liberally with soapy water until you have removed as much as possible.

4. If the stain remains, apply a laundry presoak (spot stain remover) and let stand several minutes.

5. Launder in the hottest water safe for the fabric.

CHALK

GENERAL DESCRIPTION: A soft, crumbly white stone made of compressed plankton fossils. Commonly used by teachers as a tool for communicating with students, chalk can be found in classrooms and in teachers' pockets around the world. Chalk has served a number of purposes in addition to teachers' tool—in Victorian England, milk contained chalk as an additive for aesthetic reasons.

SEASON:

This stain appears throughout the school year. It is much more rare during summer months, but those attending summer school and children fond of drawing on sidewalks are susceptible to this stain even in summer.

AREAS OF OCCURRENCE:

For educators, their seats of pants and skirts and their sweaters are common areas for this stain. However, chalk and its dust are far-reaching due to their powdery consistency, and they can therefore be found on the sleeves of jackets as well as shoes and backpacks. For students, chalk dust may be wiped almost anywhere, from socks to mittens. Additionally, the student with a naughty streak might find themself covered from head to foot in the stuff after an eraser-banging chastisement.

TIME OF OCCURRENCE:

Chalk stains almost always occur during the day, between the hours of 9 a.m. and 3 p.m., except when they occur during the aforementioned after-school punishment. Occasionally these stains may crop up on the weekends, when children take to the streets for hopscotch. You might even incur this stain in the evening, during a night class. Gymnasts, baseball pitchers, artists, and pool sharks often obtain this stain during their work hours.

VARIATIONS OF SIGNIFICANCE:

Chewable antacids

REMOVAL:

1. Shake garment outdoors or vacuum to remove as much loose chalk as possible.

2. Place fabric stain-down over an absorbent cloth and blot the back of the stain with rubbing alcohol. Replace cloth as it becomes saturated.

3. Rinse well.

4. Repeat steps 2 and 3 until you have removed as much chalk as possible.

5. Rub liquid detergent into the stain and let stand several minutes.

6. Launder according to garment label.

CORRECTION FLUID

GENERAL DESCRIPTION: A quick-drying opaque white fluid used to cover ink marks on paper. Bette Nesmith Graham, the mother of former Monkee Mike Nesmith, invented correction fluid. She later named the product Liquid Paper and, in 1979, sold the rights to the Gillette Company for $47.5 million. This product has since become a staple in desk drawers everywhere, be it in the home or in the office. Though it was mainly intended (and used) to correct typewriter errors, even in the era of the delete key correction fluid is handy for holiday cards, printed documents, and tweens painting their nails.

SEASON: Correction fluid creates stains throughout the year, but such stains may be particularly widespread during the hectic days of tax season.

AREAS OF OCCURRENCE: Stains from this helpful fluid are prevalent on the arms of collared shirts and on dresses, and any other garment suitable for office attire. Other affected areas may include tabletops, carpeting, upholstered furniture, and the cloth walls of an office cubicle.

TIME OF OCCURRENCE: Students and taxpayers prone to procrastination might encounter this stain during late-night or very early morning hours, but it is most commonly acquired from 9 a.m. to 5 p.m.

VARIATIONS OF SIGNIFICANCE: Correction tape

REMOVAL:

1. Spray both sides of fabric with WD-40™ to loosen the stain. Let stand until the stain is loosened (dab with fingers to see if any comes off).

2. Rinse well.

3. Lay stain facedown on absorbent cloth. Saturate back of stain with nail polish remover. Turn garment over and sponge surface of stain with nail polish remover. You can also substitute acetone for nail polish remover for a stronger approach; use according to manufacturer's directions.

4. Rinse well.

5. Repeat steps 3 and 4 until you have removed as much stain as possible.

6. Apply a laundry presoak (spot stain remover) and let stand several minutes.

7. Launder according to garment label.

CRAYON

GENERAL DESCRIPTION: A stick of colored wax, used for drawing or coloring. Crayons are practically synonymous with the brand name Crayola, which is a combination of the French word *craie*, "chalk" and *ola*, from "oleaginous," meaning oily. Emerson Moser, who was Crayola's senior crayon maker for more than 30 years and made over a billion crayons, revealed upon his retirement that he was mildly colorblind.

SEASON: Children and artists alike use crayons for their art projects throughout the year; however, parents generally find crayon stains on their children's clothing during the school year. Younger children are probably the most likely to experience crayon stains.

AREAS OF OCCURRENCE: Depending upon the user's level of creativity, crayons may stain sleeves of T-shirts, sweaters, and jackets, pant legs, and shoes. An art teacher might employ smocks in the classroom, so stains also appear on the fronts and sleeves of these coverings. Walls and floors are also common places to find crayon stains, especially in households containing particularly boisterous tots.

TIME OF OCCURRENCE: The hours between 9 a.m. and 3 p.m. are the most likely times to obtain this stain, though these stains aren't limited to the school day. Coloring is a favorite pastime of children all over the world, and parents are often grateful for the quiet moments in the evening when youngsters busy themselves with books and crayons. The wee hours of the night are a time when crayon stains rarely occur, though artists who use crayons might find the muse striking late into the night.

REMOVAL: *On fabric:*

1. Place stained item on absorbent paper towels. Spray each side with WD-40™, letting stand several minutes after each application.

2. Rinse well.

3. Rub dishwashing liquid into the stain with a damp cloth. Replace the cloth as it becomes saturated with crayon. Repeat until no more crayon is removed.

4. Rinse well.

5. Apply a laundry presoak (spot stain remover) and let stand several minutes.

6. Launder in the hottest water safe for the fabric.

7. If the stain remains, let dry in sunlight and repeat steps 1 through 6.

On a hard surface, such as wood, tile, or paneling:

1. Spray stain with WD-40™ to loosen the crayon, then wipe off with a paper towel. Test first in an inconspicuous area. If WD-40™ is not available, substitute non-gel toothpaste. Rub over stain, let stand 15 minutes, then wipe off. Repeat as needed.

2. Sponge the stain with dishwashing liquid and hot water.

3. Rinse with water.

GLUE, MODEL AIRPLANE

GENERAL DESCRIPTION: A strong liquid adhesive especially conducive to bonding with plastic pieces. Model-airplane cement is a solvent-type adhesive, which is actually a welding agent. It dissolves the plastics to be bonded, allowing them to join and weld before the solvent evaporates.

SEASON:

❄

Model-airplane enthusiasts are particularly active during periods of free time and when they are confined to home. Therefore, stains from this type of glue are most common during cold winter months when recreation is best kept indoors.

AREAS OF OCCURRENCE:

Those who engage in the precision work of building model airplanes rarely experience gluing accidents. However, there are times when concentration is so intense that glue spills onto a tabletop, carpet, or even shirts or pants. In extreme cases, elbows or shirt cuffs end up stuck to a tabletop or other surface.

TIME OF OCCURRENCE:

Though building model airplanes is an activity probably best left to daylight hours, when you are most likely to be completely alert, those who practice this hobby might find themselves working on a wing or a fuselage well into the wee hours. It is at these times when the potential for stain is greatest.

REMOVAL:

△

1. Blot stain with nail polish remover containing acetone, or with straight acetone. Test first for colorfastness. Do not use acetone on acetate materials or silk.

◊ 2. Rinse well.

3. Repeat steps 1 and 2 until you have removed as much stain as possible.

 4. Launder according to garment label.

GLUE, RUBBER CEMENT

GENERAL DESCRIPTION: Solid rubber dispersed in a volatile (often flammable) solvent; when the solvent evaporates, the residue is pure rubber, which acts as a flexible adhesive. Perhaps most people will remember rubber cement from grade school, where making "boogies" out of the stuff was thought to be a great prank. In fact, rubber cement's consistency is such that its stains are not as irksome as those from regular glue. A surface spread with rubber cement can easily be repositioned or removed even after the adhesive has set (this is how sticky notes are made). If the rubber cement is applied to both surfaces before they are joined, however, the bond is permanent.

SEASON: Though adults may find uses for rubber cement on occasion, schoolchildren are the primary users of this substance. Stains are thus most likely encountered during the school year.

AREAS OF OCCURRENCE: The lap area of trousers and jeans as well as the fronts of jumpers, shirts, sweaters, and jackets are candidates for this stain. Luckily, unlike other glues, rubber cement is very thick, cutting down on its ability to run down clothing and spread the stain.

TIME OF OCCURRENCE: The hours between 9 a.m. and 3 p.m. are the most likely times for this stain to occur. Occasionally, during the preparation of a project for a science fair or art class, a child may cause a rubber-cement stain after school or in the evening.

REMOVAL: 1. Use a dull knife or spoon to remove as much as possible.

2. Rub petroleum jelly into the stain and roll off as many glue pieces as possible.

3. Rub dishwashing liquid into the stain.

4. Rinse in warm water.

5. Try to peel or scrape excess glue off.

6. Repeat steps 2 through 5 until no more glue can be removed.

7. Launder in the hottest water safe for the fabric.

GLUE, WATER-BASED

GENERAL
DESCRIPTION: A strong liquid adhesive. Used for everything from kids' craft projects to postage stamps, this kind of glue can be found in any number of places. Although some glue has historically been made with animal parts, these days most glue is synthetic and therefore kosher and vegan (the exceptions are generally specialty glues, like those used to make violins and other stringed instruments). Of course, you probably shouldn't eat glue—though this isn't always easy, since it's used on lick-to-adhere stamps and envelope flaps. Most stamps these days are self-adhesive, but in 2013 a postage stamp with chocolate-flavored glue was released in Belgium.

SEASON:	Glue has its purposes year-round—it certainly has a significant presence at any crafts function at camp and school, and even at home when making collages and holiday cards with a personal touch.
AREAS OF OCCURRENCE:	Glue stains present themselves in any number of areas—shirts, shorts, pants, and uniforms are all vulnerable at one point or another. The collar and cuff areas of shirts may be at increased risk when worn by a child with an affinity for tasting and perhaps even eating the glue or paste in their elementary school classroom.
VARIATIONS OF SIGNIFICANCE:	Paste; glue stick
REMOVAL:	1. Use a dull knife or spoon to remove as much as possible.
	2. Rub petroleum jelly into the stain and roll off as many glue pieces as possible.
	3. Rub dishwashing liquid into the stain.
	4. Rinse in warm water.
	5. Try to peel or scrape excess glue off.
	6. Repeat steps 2 through 5 until no more glue can be removed.
	7. Launder in the hottest water safe for the fabric.

INK, BALLPOINT

GENERAL DESCRIPTION: Semisolid substance used for writing or printing, contained in a cartridge inside a pen in which the point is a fine ball bearing that rotates against the ink supply. In the U.K., ballpoint pens are sometimes called "biros," after the Hungarian-born journalist Laszlo Josef Biro, who invented the ball mechanism. Laszlo and his brother George patented the Biro pen in 1938. When ballpoint pens were first sold in America in 1945, they were priced at a whopping $12 apiece. Nowadays, ballpoint pens are the least expensive, though still the most popular, of all ink pens available.

SEASON:

Most people need to write every day, all year long, thus a stain incurred from the ink in ballpoints may appear at the home or the office—or in the car or outside—any day of the year.

AREAS OF OCCURRENCE:

The knees of jeans seem to be popular spots for a line of blue ink; some students might even intentionally put ink on their clothing, especially within the confines of junior high school. Another spot ink stains are generally found is on or around the breast pockets of dress shirts and suit jackets, due to the predilection of ballpoints to leak or break in the pocket. Ink spots may also be found on desks, tables, and walls.

TIME OF OCCURRENCE: There is no time of day or night when a staining of ink in a ballpoint pen will not occur. Homework, poetry, and letter-writing are activities that take place in the afternoon or the middle of the night, or any other time of day when students or authors are so motivated.

REMOVAL: *On fabric:*

1. Lay the item stain-down on an absorbent material, such as a paper towel. Soak the back of the stain with rubbing alcohol. This will push the stain through the fabric. Blot frequently.

2. Rinse well.

3. If the stain remains, repeat this process with an alcohol-based hairspray (spray the back of the stain), nail polish remover, or turpentine until you find the right method.

4. Rinse well after each treatment.

5. Rub a liquid enzyme detergent into the stain and let stand several minutes.

6. Launder according to garment label.

On a hard surface, such as wood, paneling, or tile:

1. Wipe with damp cloth or sponge.

2. If the stain remains, wipe with rubbing alcohol or nail polish remover.

3. Rinse surface with water.

INK, PERMANENT

GENERAL DESCRIPTION: A non-removable, non-erasable fluid used for writing or printing. Permanent ink creates stains that are difficult indeed—the substance's very existence depends upon its tenacity. Lab workers can spend years developing formulas that will be indelible, and marketing copy highlights this feature as the selling point that will make consumers part with their money.

SEASON:

☀

Permanent ink is a stain without season—it is not bound by weather or month. You may notice an increased risk during the summer months, when you are more likely to label boxes for a move or make signs advertising a yard or garage sale.

AREAS OF
OCCURRENCE:

Shirts, especially sleeves and cuffs, as well as pants are prime targets for this difficult stain. If children or unobservant employees get a hold of a permanent marker, walls and whiteboards may also be at risk.

TIME OF
OCCURRENCE:

Ink stains are probable at any time indelible ink pens are in use—most likely during daylight hours.

SPECIAL NOTE:

This stain needs immediate treatment. Check the ink manufacturer to see if a particular solvent is recommended; use this before employing the stain removal steps that follow.

REMOVAL:

On fabric:

1. Place fabric on absorbent cloth and blot the stain with rubbing alcohol. Replace cloth underneath as it becomes saturated with alcohol and ink. Continue until no more ink can be removed.

2. Rinse well.

3. If the stain remains, blot with either acetone (except on acetates) or turpentine. Test first for colorfastness. Replace cloth underneath as it becomes saturated with acetone and ink. Continue until no more ink can be removed.

4. Rinse well.

5. Apply a laundry presoak (spot stain remover) and let stand several minutes.

6. Launder according to garment label.

7. If the stain remains, soak in milk or rub it with white, non-gel toothpaste.

8. Rinse well.

9. Repeat steps 7 and 8 as needed.

10. Apply a laundry presoak (spot stain remover) and let stand several minutes.

11. Launder according to garment label.

On a hard surface, such as wood, paneling, or tile:

1. Dampen a cloth with nail polish remover or rubbing alcohol and wipe stain.

2. Rinse surface with water.

3. Repeat steps 1 and 2 as needed.

INK, WATER-BASED

GENERAL DESCRIPTION: A fluid used for writing or printing that is made from a base of water with pigment added. Water-based ink is the easiest type of ink to remove from clothing and skin, but doesn't have the varied uses that permanent ink does. It is often used in marking pens, and comes in a variety of colors.

<table>
<tr><td>

SEASON:

</td><td>

Art projects are assigned year-round, but especially during the school year, making this stain marginally more likely between September and June.

</td></tr>
</table>

SEASON:

Art projects are assigned year-round, but especially during the school year, making this stain marginally more likely between September and June.

AREAS OF OCCURRENCE:

The most common place you see water-based ink stains is on the fingers and hands of someone who has recently completed a drawing or created a home-made birthday card. This substance will easily find its way from the hands onto clothing; the lap areas of jeans and slacks as well as the sleeves and fronts of T-shirts, turtlenecks, and sweaters are the most vulnerable. Other places this stain is likely to appear include tabletops, desks, chairs, walls, and tile flooring.

REMOVAL:

On fabric:

1. Lay the stain down on an absorbent paper towel. Soak another clean white cloth in rubbing alcohol and dab the other side of the stain. (You can also use water in place of alcohol; use whichever removes the most ink.) Replace the cloth underneath if it becomes soaked. Repeat until you have removed as much ink as possible.

2. Rinse the back of the stain well with water.

3. Rub a liquid laundry detergent into the stain and let stand several minutes.

4. Launder the fabric in the hottest water safe for the fabric.

5. If the stain does not disappear completely, repeat steps 1 through 3, then place item in direct sunlight for several hours to bleach remaining color.

On a hard surface, such as wood, paneling, or tile:

1. Wipe with damp cloth or sponge.

2. If the stain remains, wipe with rubbing alcohol or nail polish remover.

3. Rinse surface with water.

PENCIL

GENERAL DESCRIPTION:

A cylindrical writing implement, generally made of wood but sometimes plastic, which contains a mark-depositing material like graphite, charcoal, or colored wax. Pencils are the implements children use when learning to write letters and numbers; from preschool into adulthood, a pencil is the tool of choice when completing an assignment like a test, a math problem, a drawing, a crossword puzzle, or any other task that may require erasure. In contemporary times, most pencils come equipped with a bit of pink rubber on the top; before this was a common practice, graphite pencil was erased using bread crumbs.

SEASON:

Pencil stains are without a doubt most common during the months when children are in school. Teachers, students, and even parents may find themselves unwitting victims of this stain. During these months there is a heightened risk at the time of standardized testing, when the use of a number 2 pencil is always required.

AREAS OF OCCURRENCE:	Stray pencil markings can stain school uniforms, pockets, or backpacks. Engineers' or editors' shirt pockets are high-risk areas as well. Beware of the pencil sharpener—this nasty device will spread pencil shavings and, in turn, pencil stains to seemingly unreachable areas, such as socks and pant cuffs.
TIME OF OCCURRENCE:	Pencil stains are wily—they belong to the class of stains wherein the victim might not discover their misfortune for hours, or perhaps even days, after the event, especially when the affected area is inside a book bag or purse.
REMOVAL:	1. Erase gently with a clean eraser.
	2. If the stain remains, apply a laundry presoak (spot stain remover).
	3. Launder according to garment label.

GLOSSARY

ABSORBENT CLOTH:	A material, such as paper towel, sponge, or terrycloth (washcloths or towels), that collects excess stain and liquid. Select a cloth that does not have added perfumes or dyes if possible.
ABSORBENT POWDER:	A powder, such as talcum powder, baking soda, cornstarch, or salt, that absorbs excess liquid from grease and other stains.
ACETONE:	A liquid solvent that is helpful in treating nail polish and correction fluid stains. Acetone–based nail polish remover is a readily available form of this solvent. Never use acetone on acetate materials. Test before applying. Caution: Use according to manufacturer's directions. AVAILABLE: **drugstore, hardware store, grocery store**
ALCOHOL, RUBBING (OR ISOPROPYL):	A liquid solvent that is helpful in removing ballpoint ink, chalk, and grass stains. Test before applying. Caution: Use according to manufacturer's directions. AVAILABLE: **drugstore, grocery store**
AMMONIA:	A colorless gas that is easily absorbed by water; it is sold diluted in water. Helpful in restoring color damaged by bleaches, as well as in treating vinegar stains. Test before applying; generally not safe for silks and wools. Caution: Use according to manufacturer's directions. AVAILABLE: **drugstore, grocery store**
BAKING SODA (BICARBONATE OF SODA):	An absorbent powder that is nontoxic and nonabrasive. It is often combined with water to form an absorbent paste and is good for treating greasy stains. AVAILABLE: **grocery store**

BAR OR NATURAL SOAP:	Any white bathroom soap. Select brands without added moisturizers, perfumes, and dyes. Using a bar or natural soap can set certain stains; read all directions thoroughly. AVAILABLE: **drugstore, grocery store**
BLEACH:	Generally, a chemical that removes most color stains. Mild bleaches include white vinegar, lemon juice, hydrogen peroxide, and sunlight. Stronger bleaches, which are readily available and are labeled as "bleach," may contain fabric-weakening chlorine and should be used as a last resort. Chlorine bleach is generally not safe for wool and silk. Test first for colorfastness. Non-chlorine bleaches are also available. Caution: Use according to manufacturer's directions. AVAILABLE: **drugstore, grocery store, natural-food store**
BLOT:	To dry or soak up with an absorbent cloth. When blotting a stain with water or other cleaning agent, always blot from the outside edge of the stain and work into the center. This prevents the stain from spreading and forming rings.
BORAX:	A powdered mineral compound with antibacterial, antiseptic, and whitening properties. Also called sodium tetraborate or sodium borate. AVAILABLE: **drugstore, hardware store**
CARPET SPOTTER:	A liquid spray or foaming cream often advertised as a quick carpet cleaner. Caution: Use according to manufacturer's directions. AVAILABLE: **drugstore, grocery store**
CHEESECLOTH:	Thin, loosely woven cotton gauze. AVAILABLE: **grocery store**

CLUB SODA:	Carbonated water with some dissolved minerals. Also called mineral water. Cold water or unflavored seltzer (carbonated water) can be used in its place. Note: Club soda is not the same as tonic water, which contains sugars that will caramelize and form new stains once heat is applied. AVAILABLE: **grocery store**
COLD WATER:	Water at the temperature of ice water, or the coldest tap water.
COLORFAST:	Having colors or dyes that do not run or bleed. Testing for colorfastness is recommended before using any kind of bleach or strong cleaning product. To test, apply the cleaning agent to an inconspicuous area of the garment, such as an inside seam, and dab with an absorbent cloth. If colors run, do not use the cleaning agent on the garment.
COMMERCIAL DYE REMOVER:	Products that are helpful in restoring colors that have run onto other garments. Caution: Use according to manufacturer's directions. AVAILABLE: **drugstore, grocery store**
CORNSTARCH:	Also called cornflour in the U.K. A starch made from corn that can be used as an absorbent powder. AVAILABLE: **grocery store**
DISHWASHING LIQUID:	Any basic dishwashing liquid. Select brands that are phosphate-free and do not have added dyes or perfumes. AVAILABLE: **drugstore, grocery store**
DRY-CLEANING FLUID:	An oil solvent that is helpful in treating oily, greasy stains and is safe for nonwashables. Caution: Use according to manufacturer's directions. AVAILABLE: **drugstore**

EMERY BOARD:	Small flat board with an abrasive texture, which is normally used for filing nails but can also help remove scorch marks. AVAILABLE: **drugstore, beauty supply store**
ENZYME DETERGENT:	A laundry detergent containing enzymes that "eat" protein stains. Enzyme detergents are also called "digestants." Note: Animal-derived materials such as wool and silk are proteins, so never use enzyme detergents on these fibers. AVAILABLE: **drugstore, grocery store, natural-food store**
EUCALYPTUS OIL:	Oil derived from the eucalyptus plant. Test before applying. AVAILABLE: **drugstore, natural-food store**
GLYCERIN:	A naturally produced emollient that is made synthetically or from plant or animal sources, which can be found in liquid or solid form. AVAILABLE: **drugstore, natural-food store**
HOT WATER:	Water at a temperature at which you cannot comfortably keep your hand submerged. Never use hot water on protein stains; the heat can set them.
HYDROGEN PEROXIDE (3%):	A mild bleach. Test first for colorfastness. Hydrogen peroxide loses strength over time and when exposed to sunlight, so purchase in small quantities and keep in a cabinet. AVAILABLE: **drugstore, grocery store**
LAUNDRY PRESOAK:	A spot stain remover applied prior to laundering; sold as a liquid, gel, or solid stick. AVAILABLE: **drugstore, grocery store, natural food store**
LEMON JUICE:	A mild bleach. Test first for colorfastness. AVAILABLE: **grocery store**

LAUNDRY DETERGENT:	Any basic laundry cleanser. Select phosphate-free brands that do not have added dyes and perfumes. AVAILABLE: **drugstore, grocery store, natural-food store**
LUKEWARM WATER:	Water you can comfortably keep your hand in; typically the temperature of bathwater.
MEAT TENDERIZER:	A powder that contains enzymes that help break down proteins. AVAILABLE: **grocery store**
NAIL POLISH REMOVER:	A mild solvent. Select brands without added dyes or perfumes. AVAILABLE: **drugstore**
NON-GEL TOOTHPASTE:	A pasty toothpaste that can serve as an absorbent powder when applied to a stain. AVAILABLE: **drugstore, grocery store, natural-food store**
OILY LUBRICANT:	Car-part lubricant that is helpful in "loosening" stains or solids from fabric. Caution: Use according to manufacturer's directions. AVAILABLE: **hardware store**
PAINT AND VARNISH REMOVER:	A solvent used to remove acrylic- and oil-based paint stains. Select an odorless brand. Caution: Use according to manufacturer's directions. AVAILABLE: **hardware store**
RINSE:	To flush the back of a stain with water to remove as much of a staining or cleaning agent as possible. If water temperature is not clearly stated in stain removal directions, use lukewarm water. Never rinse with hot water unless stated in directions.
RUST REMOVER:	A liquid solvent that is helpful in removing rust stains and some dirt or mud stains. Caution: Use according

to manufacturer's directions. AVAILABLE: **hardware store**

SOLUTION: A mixture of one or more substances with a solvent. For example, liquid laundry detergent and water (a solvent) form a solution.

SOLVENT: A material, like water, that is capable of dissolving another substance.

SPONGE: To moisten with an absorbent cloth.

TALCUM POWDER: An absorbent powder that is helpful in treating ointment, salad dressing, and other greasy stains. AVAILABLE: **drugstore, grocery store**

TILE CLEANER: Liquid or foaming product for use in the bathroom. Caution: Use according to manufacturer's directions. AVAILABLE: **drugstore, grocery store, natural-food store**

TURPENTINE: A solvent derived from pine oil that is used as a thinner for tough grease stains such as tar and asphalt, as well as for oil-based paints. Caution: Use according to manufacturer's directions. AVAILABLE: **hardware store**

VINEGAR, WHITE: A solution of 5 percent acetic acid that can be used as a mild bleach. Test first for colorfastness. AVAILABLE: **grocery store**

INDEX

A
adhesives, 230–32

ammonia, 122

animal fats, 45–48

antiperspirants, 207–9

asphalt, 181–84

avocado, 14–15

B
baby food, 15–16

baby formula, 54–55

baby oil, 204–5

baked beans, 17–18

baking soda, 30–31, 47, 87, 88, 92

ballpoint ink, 243–44

barbecue sauce, 70–71

bathroom and beauty products, 203–7; baby oil, 204–5; blush or rouge, 205–7; deodorants or antiperspirants, 207–9; eyeliner or eye shadow, 209–11; foundation, 211–12; lip balm, 212–14; lipstick, 214–15; lotion, hand, body, or suntan, 215–18; mascara, 218–20; nail polish, 220–22; ointment, 222–24; perfume, 224–26; toothpaste, 226–27

beauty products. *See* bathroom and beauty products

beer, 105–6

beet, 18–20

berries, 24–27

beverages, 103–19; beer, 105–6; coffee, 107–9; liquor and mixed drinks, 104–5; soft drinks, 109–11; tea, 112–14; wine, red, 116–18; wine, white, 118–19

bleach, 123–24

blood, 188–90

blush, 205–7

bodily functions, 187–201; blood, 188–90; excrement,
    190–92; ring around the collar, 192–93; semen, 192–93;
    sweat, 194–96; urine, 196–98; vomit, 198–201

body lotion, 215–18

broccoli, 20–21

burn marks, 147–49

butter, 55–56

C

cabbage, red, 22–23

candle wax, 158–59

caramel, 71–73

carbon paper, 232–33

carrot, 23–24

chalk, 233–35

charcoal, 164–65

cheese, 57–58

chocolate, 73–75

coffee, 107–9

collar, ring around the, 192–93

colorfastness, testing for, 9

colors, running, 124–25

condiments. *See* sauces and condiments

cooking oil, 86–88

copier toner, 232–33

cornstarch, 47, 87, 92

correction fluid, 235–36

crayon, 237–38

cream, 61–62

smoke, 151–53

soft drinks, 109–11

soot, 151–53

sour cream, 64–66

soy sauce, 94–95

spinach, 36–37

squash, 37–38

stains: identifying, 10; removal tips, 9

steak sauce, 70–71

suntan lotion, 215–18

sweat, 194–96

sweet potato, 34–36

syrup, maple, 81–82

T

tar, 181–84

tarnish, 153–54

tea, 112–14

testing for colorfastness, 9

tobacco, 154–56

tomato, 38–40

tomato juice, 114–16

tomato sauce, 95–97

toothpaste, 37, 226–27

tuna fish, 50–51

U

urine, 196–98

V

vegetable oil, 86–88

vegetables. *See* fruits and vegetables